Future Issues
in
Health Care

**SOCIAL POLICY AND
THE RATIONING
OF MEDICAL SERVICES**

David Mechanic

THE FREE PRESS
A Division of Macmillan Publishing Co., Inc.
NEW YORK

Collier Macmillan Publishers
LONDON

THE FREE PRESS
A Division of Macmillan Publishing Co., Inc.
866 Third Avenue, New York, N.Y. 10022

Collier Macmillan Canada, Ltd.

Library of Congress Catalog Card Number: 78-63413

Printed in the United States of America

printing number

1 2 3 4 5 6 7 8 9 10

Library of Congress Cataloging in Publication Data

Mechanic, David
    Future issues in health care.

    Bibliography: p.
    1. Medical care—United States.   2. Medical
policy—United States.   3. Social medicine—United
States.   4. Medical care—Research.   I. Title.
RA395.A3M416   362.1'0973   78-63413
ISBN 0-02-920710-X

For Linda

Contents

Foreword *by David A. Hamburg*   vii

Preface   xi

Part I   Introduction and Analytic Framework

    1 Introduction   3

    2 Controlling the Costs of Medical Care:
       Short-Range and Long-Range Alternatives   10

Part II   Patients' Health Behavior and the Medical Marketplace

    3 Changing Individual Health Behavior:
       Rhetoric and Reality   25

    4 Making the Medical Marketplace Work:
       Psychological Considerations   38

Part III Problems in Long-Term Care and Mental Health

    5 Some Problems in Long-Term Care   51

    6 Community Integration of the Mentally Ill   64

    7 Mental-Health Benefits under
       National Health Insurance   75

Part IV   Social Regulation of Medical Care

  8 Theories of Rationing   91

  9 Patients' Rights and the
     Regulation of Medical Practice   104

Part V   Health Services and Behavioral Research

 10 Monitoring the Health-Care System:
     Health-Services Research   125

 11 Behavioral Research and Health:
     The Need for a Broad View   137

 12 Behavioral Research and Health:
     The Study of Health and Illness Behavior   146

 13 The Politics of Change:
     The Potential for Reform   159

     References   177

     Index   189

Foreword

To speak of rationing in the context of medical care is uncomfortable, even painful. Are we, in this great, generous, and affluent country, to limit the availability of tools for saving human lives and diminishing human suffering? At first glance, it is almost unthinkable.

Yet more and more these days, the nearly taboo word "rationing" passes the lips of those seriously concerned with medical care. And even more often than the word, the concept is in the air—and indeed in the practice of health care.

So David Mechanic, in his typically bold and forthright way, has decided to speak the unspeakable, to bring the issue into the open so that it can be treated analytically. His purpose is clarification, differentiation, searching consideration of whatever "rationing" may mean, how it occurs and might occur in the future. His examination of these issues constitutes a substantial contribution to health policy.

Rationing usually refers to a policy intended to allocate scarce resources systematically in ways that tend to conserve those resources and distribute them fairly.

Much difference of opinion exists, on the basis of past experience as well as abstract principles, as to what constitutes a just basis for distribution of scarce resources—e.g., to each according to merit, to each according to contribution, to each according to need, or similar treatment for similar cases. Each of these approaches has different consequences. These matters are especially difficult to resolve in practice in a large, heterogeneous society such as that of the United States; serious efforts must be made to take into account multiple values and competing interests.

As we move into a new era of debate on rationing of health care, it will be useful to clarify different aims of rationing and the probable consequences of each aim—e.g., the control of cost or the best use of resources or equity in care.

When all services considered necessary (in terms of social consensus or professional criteria) cannot be provided for all who need them, then rationing occurs whether it is intended or not. How stringent the rationing becomes depends on social responses, including (1) the ability to produce services more economically or to devise acceptable substitutes, (2) the reduction of demand by preventing illness, diminishing public expectations of medical care, or narrowing the area of medical responsibility, and (3) changes in willingness to invest in medical care in private and/or public sectors.

This is not a completely new problem by any means. Traditionally, health-care services have been limited in availability by relative shortages of manpower and facilities, by price, and by practical barriers such as distance and waiting time. These factors have usually had considerably more impact on the poor and socially isolated than on the fortunate mainstream of society.

In this book, Mechanic explores both implicit and explicit rationing. Implicit rationing involves limiting the resources available for health care, e.g., by fixed prospective budgets or by restrictions on facilities. This is intended to put pressure on health-care providers to make allocation choices; typically this approach does not specify the basis on which those choices are to be made or the types of services to be provided. It assumes that, by limiting resources, well-informed health professionals will carefully work out priority decisions. In reality, such judgments vary by type of training, type of practice setting, community power relations, or other factors. Thus, sophisticated patients are likely to get more service than less educated population groups. Serious questions of equity may arise. Concerns have been expressed that such systems make physicians less responsive to patients or otherwise adversely affect the doctor-patient relationship.

Explicit rationing involves administrative decisions regarding limitations on what services will be provided or covered under health insurance. It includes such mechanisms as advance review of expensive procedures and concurrent utilization review. Explicit rationing departs in some respects from traditions of physician autonomy and clinical responsibility. Inequities may occur in allocation decisions through strong political pressures. Moreover, guidelines and regulations could be developed that do not adequately take into account the realities of clinical situations and the variability of patients' needs. On the other hand, explicit rationing shifts rationing responsibility from health professionals to an independent third party, and thus may have less danger for the physician-patient relationship than implicit rationing schemes.

Mechanic not only delineates more clearly the nature of implicit and explicit rationing; he also seeks objectively to consider the probable advantages and limitations of each. He does not follow ideological stereotypes, nor does he shrink from complex issues.

The problems considered in this book are at the frontiers of health policy. Alternative ways of rationing health care deserve the kind of careful attention Mechanic has given them here—not only in the immediate future, but for many years to come. The power of diagnostic, therapeutic, and preventive interventions—based on the truly unprecedented advances in scientific understanding—is growing rapidly. So too is the complexity and expense of the system.

Any system of national health insurance is likely to involve a mix of rationing by implicit and explicit methods. The aim is to find a mix of techniques that are responsive to patient need, that protect responsible flexibility of health professionals in clinical judgment, and that are prudent in public and private expenditures. The choices will be difficult, and hardships will occur. Advances in knowledge on all levels pertinent to health care will be needed to deal reasonably and fairly with these dilemmas. The gaps in knowledge delineated in this book cry out for strengthening of health - services research, built on the foundations of basic science and clinical investigation.

Thus, David Mechanic's penetrating analysis not only helps to clarify pressing current issues, but it will also stimulate badly needed inquiry into the foundations of health care. It deserves the thoughtful attention of all those seriously interested in health policy.

David A. Hamburg
President, Institute of Medicine
National Academy of Sciences

Preface

The growing cost of medical care frightens thoughtful people and results in many frantic efforts on the part of policymakers and administrators to get some handle on the system or nonsystem as the case might be. The financial issues have become so acute that they tend to push all other matters into the background as policymakers search for mechanisms to contain costs. The immediate pressures on programs and administrators do not make for careful and searching inquiry; instead they encourage short-range and often shortsighted attempts that give the appearance that something is being done. Cost containment is no trivial problem either practically or intellectually. Costs are unlikely to be contained through approaches that fail to take account of the larger forces affecting the medical-care process.

Containing costs is only part of the problem. The challenge is to do so while providing reasonable access to medical care that is effective and humane. If the issue were simply cost, the solution would be simple, because all we would need to do is reduce budgets. Achieving tighter allocations, however, without significantly limiting access or high-quality and sensitive care, and doing so in a politically acceptable manner, is a baffling challenge. Although there is much puffery around one or another solution, the fact is that no one really has much confidence that we know what to do or that we could do it if we knew.

In short, the problem of the costs of medical care is here to stay in one form or another. The problem is not simply an issue of greedy practitioners, too many hospital beds, or inefficient practices, although all exist. The problem more basically arises from the public's rising demands and expectations, the growth of knowledge, and the development of new technologies. There is no sign that these influences are likely to diminish in the future.

In this book I examine cost-containment problems, but in the context of impending problems of health need and medical care. If there is a single thread that ties these discussions, it is the importance of understanding behavior in designing and implementing social policy, for it is the perceptions and responses of those affected that will ultimately determine the fate of public policy. Unlike many currently fashionable theorists on medical care, I raise more problems than I solve and remain skeptical of a utopian solution. I also am optimistic, however, that significant progress has been made and that further reform is possible. Controlling cost—like increasing access, improving the capacity of the care system, and providing sensitive and high-quality care—will come not by one major thrust but by long-term efforts to understand how to affect the behavior of patients and physicians and how to design incentives that will not be diverted or perverted.

In this book, I use the term "rationing" to describe alternative methods of allocating limited medical resources. I know from experience that this term elicits anger from some physicians who have the notion that rationing is a future threat rather than a reality describing the present and the past. I consciously have chosen the more inciting term because I believe it is more honest to describe things as they really are. The choice of terms is often a means of deception. Middle-class Americans, for example, believe that it is only the poor who receive rent subsidies, rarely defining the deductions of mortgage interest on their taxes as such a subsidy. Such self-deceptions in the aggregate have a distorting effect on rational discussions of social policy. We all should accept the fact that medical care in America, as elsewhere, is rationed.

Some of the chapters have been previously published. I thank the *New England Journal of Medicine* (298[February 2, 1978]:249- 54) for permission to reproduce "Approaches to Controlling the Costs of Medical Care: Short-Range and Long-Range Alternatives" and the *American Journal of Public Health* (68[May 1978]:482- 88) for permission to republish "Considerations in the Design of Mental-Health Benefits under National Health Insurance."

This book was written with the support of a John Simon Guggenheim Memorial Foundation Fellowship with additional assistance from the Research Committee of the Graduate School of the University of Wisconsin—Madison and from the Robert Wood Johnson Foundation. During this period I was a Visiting Fellow at the Department of Sociology and the Woodrow Wilson School of Public and International Affairs at Princeton University. I am grateful to all these institutions for the opportunities provided.

Linda Aiken read the manuscript in draft and made many helpful suggestions, but most of all encouraged me to continue when I was frustrated with it. As in the past, I am particularly grateful to have two extraordinary assistants—Ann Wallace and Lorraine Borsuk—who typed the manuscript, checked references, assisted in proofreading, and did a variety of other tasks. I have come to trust them more than I trust myself. As is customary, I take the responsibility for all errors but, I hope, for some telling points as well.

Introduction and Analytic Framework

1 | Introduction

Health care is an elaborate social system, affected by attitudes, values, and ideologies as much as by profiles of illness, economics, and technology. How the patient perceives and uses the medical-care system and how professionals mobilize to perform their tasks are in part consequences of social and cultural trends, modes of child rearing, and patterns of professional socialization. From a purely rational point of view, patients should seek care primarily when they are ill or when there is a tangible benefit to be gained from a medical encounter. And physician response should reflect the complexity and severity of the patient's problem, the efficacy and cost effectiveness of alternative interventions, and the medical need for varying types of medical procedures and facilities. While all these factors are relevant, they fail to explain by themselves the decision-making processes that actually take place. Whether in accounting for the reasons that the patient seeks medical care or the physician's decision to hospitalize the patient, it is necessary to take social forces and psychological processes into account. If patient and physician behavior are formed by sociocultural processes as well as by medical factors, then these must be considered in effective policy formulation and administration. Policies designed simply on rational assumptions are likely to miss their mark in successfully altering behavior.

Decisions on the allocation of medical care are likely to reflect existing social values and political pressures. In American society the marketplace is viewed as the appropriate mechanism for distributing most goods and services, reflecting strong beliefs in individual autonomy and economic freedom. In the case of medical care as in the case of education, there are strong competing beliefs among large segments of the population that life and health are precious rights that should not be rationed by the marketplace and the ability to pay, but should be distributed on some more equitable basis such as need. Because some aspects of medicine deal with life-and-death decisions and because medicine is often related to the experience of suffering, it is commonly argued that people have a "right to health care." Whether medicine is truly different from other goods and services is not really the point. To the extent that the public defines it as a special case it is one.

However a community decides about the appropriate way to allocate health care and whatever the problems in achieving accept-ability of these means, problems still remain in translating desired intentions into reality. The design of an implementation process must take into account the fact that the relevant actors, whether patients or professionals, have their own needs, desires, and inclina-tions and their own agendas, shaped by cultural settings, situational pressures, and social relationships. They may thwart, manipulate, or distort any system that is introduced unless they regard the system as legitimate and equitable.

While issues of allocation are usually posed in a dramatic way—such as who will get the scarce kidney or access to hemodialysis—medical care is a mix of services, some of a lifesaving nature but most routine. Much of the mix may have limited benefit and consume considerable expenditures, but service benefits are not easily disag-gregated, and access to one type of service may be the pathway to the next. Although in theory we would want to separate the truly valuable services from the rest, this remains an insuperable problem. Beyond some obvious cases, there is much disagreement among physicians as to what works, or even the criteria to arrive at such a judgment.

The solution, we are repeatedly told, is the randomized clinical trial (Cochrane 1972), but such studies are difficult to execute, and frequently it is difficult to know for sure what practical implications can be drawn from them. Unless study results are relatively unequiv-ocal, neither professionals nor the public is easily convinced, and there may be strong economic pressures as well that reinforce current practice. The companies marketing specific products and tech-nologies have a stake in their continued use, and professionals are reluctant to forgo techniques that they have invested a great deal of effort in learning unless they are fully convinced of their lack of value. Moreover, the location of the clinician in the treatment pro-cess is likely to reinforce conceptions that particular treatments work.

regardless of the facts. Many patients show improvement or some remission of symptoms for a time whatever the therapy, and there is a strong interest on the part of both patients and doctors to believe that the therapy being provided is efficacious. Also, patients continue to demand certain types of services regardless of their demonstrated value, and physicians often find it difficult to refuse.

Alternative approaches to the problems of allocation of medical care are the private marketplace and the planning process. After two decades of growth of health insurance, government programming, and social regulation, we have neither an adequately functioning medical marketplace nor an effective planning process. Although the character of the medical encounter and the dominance of the physician over the marketplace make an effective market unlikely in any case, recent trends have obliterated any effectiveness that price rationing may have had on the consumption and provision of medical care. Similarly, the planning process still lacks legitimacy in the minds of many relevant participants, and both planners and federal administrators have moved very cautiously in attempts to structure medical care, and when they have moved, they have worked primarily at the margins.

Present dilemmas are largely old problems in new forms. Although we have made significant progress in increasing access to medical care in the last decade (Mechanic 1978a: 198-202), we still face major problems in bringing adequate medical care to many rural areas and to the inner city. We continue to have profound problems of distribution of health resources and particularly medical manpower, not only in terms of geography but also in terms of specialty balance. We continue to need more primary-care practitioners able and willing to care for the broad and ordinary problems of illness in the population, which constitute the major part of the illness burden. New knowledge and technology continue to bring new and costly possibilities to the forefront, and as the number of aged persons in the population increases, the population will require more services per capita because of the age structure. In 1975, for example, persons over sixty-five constituted one-tenth of the population but consumed almost three-tenths of total health-care expenditures. More than half of these expenditures were paid by the federal government. It is estimated that within fifty years the proportion of aged people in the population will double, and the possibilities in the future of prolonging life and replacing body parts will be staggering.

Physicians have been trained to do all that is possible to assist the patient, and with the growth of insurance and other third-party payment, the costs have risen enormously with no plateau in sight.

The decade of the 1960s brought increased government involvement in medical affairs as well as in other sectors. Medicare and Medicaid involved enormous resources, straining both federal and state budgets. The basic notion was that the private sector was reasonably sound. What was needed was entitlement and funding for services, and the existing structure could do the rest. While these programs brought some real gains and improved health for the old and the poor, they also served to reinforce many of the irrationalities and absurdities characteristic of the provision of health-care services. With increased money and open-ended budgeting came serious inflation, a proliferation of both needed and unneeded services, and profiteering of various kinds. Although these federal programs took the rap, the reality is that they primarily focused attention on abuses that were not unique to Medicare and Medicaid but characterized the ordinary way of doing business in the health sector as a whole. Because these were public programs, they were more open to scrutiny and criticism, but the problems themselves were rampant.

The approach in the 1960s was to spend money without interfering in any basic way in the structure of the health-care system. Unwilling to tackle existing interest groups by confronting core issues that would involve considerable acrimony, public administrators spent vast amounts of money in increasing entitlement or developing new programs on the theory that benefits would trickle down to those who needed help. As there was increasing evidence that federal efforts were not having the desired effect in achieving more balanced physician distribution or a better balance between primary-care physicians and specialists, congressional and legislative efforts became more targeted toward achieving specific objectives, but there remained a fear or unwillingness to attack these problems at their core (Lewis, Fein, and Mechanic 1976). In the case of physician distribution, for example, efforts were made to establish new medical schools and increase class size on the assumption that the market then would force more physicians into underdoctored areas. The result was the buildup of a possible future surplus of physicians but no significant distributional change. Although the Congress is becoming more forceful in its efforts to deal with such intractable problems as physician distribution, there remains considerable reluctance to implement the types of incentives that are likely to work.

Neoconservative and radical critiques of our health-care system use different language, but they have come to remarkably similar conclusions about the limits of reform. The neoconservatives argue that democratic pluralist politics requires a broad consensus for change, and if we are to adhere to our values of personal freedom, noncoerciveness, and political compromise, we will not be able to induce physicians into unattractive geographic areas, get them to work with "less attractive" clients, or encourage them to practice in a way they find less personally satisfying (Ginzberg 1977). In essence, the neoconservatives argue, limited reform is the price we must pay for our political system. The radical critique similarly argues that significant reform is impossible because the existing interests are unwilling to yield their influence, resources, and control and will thwart programs that threaten their position (Alford 1975). These interests are not immune to change as long as they have something to gain. The cost of significant reform, however, becomes exorbitant because changes must be built around existing interests rather than reconstituting the nature of the system itself. Both views feed a strong pessimism about future progress.

Just as the 1960s was the decade of big new spending programs, the 1970s has become the decade of new regulation. As the cost crisis mounts in medical care, policymakers seek to find means to control their financing obligations. There are limits on available funds to be invested in medical care, and it seems evident that the approach of the 1960s will not fundamentally change the medical mode of doing business. Increasingly, thus, government has turned to regulation, attempting to deal with each new problem as it arises by developing rules and bureaucratic processes of decision making. The approach to regulation, as with spending, has been incremental and in response to perceived problems, resulting in a proliferation of piecemeal regulatory processes that are expensive, poorly designed, and largely ineffective. Legislation has developed new and expensive structures—professional standards review organizations, health-systems agencies, certificates of need—and the receipt of federal monies is increasingly attached to a wide range of guidelines, rules, and reporting procedures. While these regulatory devices are structured to deal with real problems, and while each may have a reasonable logic behind it, their complexity and accumulation impose significant economic costs as well as frustrations and lowered morale. It is a remarkable fact that in trying to preserve the mirage of a "private medical-care sector" we have developed more regulation and cumbersome bureaucratic procedures than would be necessary for a completely nationalized system. The amount of regulation in comparison to the English National Health Service is staggering, and the typical private doctor in the United States feels the heavy hand of bureaucracy far more than his British counterpart.

Regulation, of course, exists to achieve worthy objectives. Much of the difficulty arises because of conflicts in such objectives and because regulation is designed on a problem-by-problem basis that often fails to examine the total impact of the regulatory process. Regulation that lacks legitimacy tends to be readily manipulated and distorted and often has effects quite different from those originally intended. As with any other social intervention, regulatory efforts must be considered carefully in terms of their costs as well as their benefits, and in regard to unanticipated and perverse effects as well as desired ones.

In this book I focus on some future problems in the health-care sector. My object is to look at policymaking in terms of the behavior of those affected so that political and social options become clearer. I hope that the book will contribute to assisting persons concerned with policy and administration to consider how legislation and regulation are received by those who are its objects, and how they are likely to respond. Policy is a process of attempting to affect the behavior of individuals. Thus, the way it is designed and implemented is crucial. To the extent that it is insensitive to cultural and social norms and to the aspirations and fears of individuals, it is likely to have effects other than intended, and often perverse.

The book begins with a general discussion of cost containment, raising both long-range and immediate possibilities for curtailing escalating expenditures. In a sense chapter 2 serves as an analytic outline for the remainder of the book, which elaborates on various points only briefly considered here. Part II considers health behavior and the behavior of patients, examining such issues as preventive health patterns and the way patients relate to the medical marketplace. This discussion is based on the premise that effective medical policy requires an understanding of patient behavior and an appreciation of the many gaps in our knowledge as to what motivates consumer responsibility for health.

Two of the most difficult problems in health policy are in the areas of mental illness and long-term care. They are areas of major analytic and policy debate and are prognostic of even larger problems in the future as the number of old people or those with chronic handicaps rises. Using this area as a prototype, in Part III I discuss such problems as developing functional alternatives to medical care, developing new institutional infrastructures and the difficulties involved, and the way that national health insurance offers potentialities for large gains but also for difficulties unless we remain alert to many special problems.

Part IV of the book deals with the development of regulatory policies in the health field. In this section I discuss the rationing of medical care in greater detail and some strategies toward developing meaningful regulation. In part V I discuss the role of health-services research and what it can and cannot contribute to policy formulation and implementation in the future. I also review research needs in behavioral research, illustrating the types of approach necessary through a detailed discussion of research on illness behavior. The book concludes with some personal comments on the politics of change in health care, drawing on some of my own experiences as an involved actor in as well as a student of health affairs.

2

Controlling the Costs of Medical Care: Short-Range and Long-Range Alternatives

The containment of the increasing costs of medical care has become of highest priority to government in the United States as well as in many other Western nations. Medical-care spending in 1977 in the United States consumed $163 billion and almost 9 percent of the GNP, and all projections for the future suggest that health-care expenditures will require increasing proportions of both the GNP and governmental budgets. There is no absolute ceiling on how much expenditure for medical care the nation can afford, but there is great skepticism in government and elsewhere that marginal increases in the health-care budget provide adequate benefits compared with similar investments in other sectors. With large budgetary pressures on federal, state, and local governments, it is inevitable that greater energies will be given to controlling increased expenditure.

Although the concept of rationing medical care has an odious ring to many ears, rationing of care has always been the norm in the United States and elsewhere (Mechanic 1977a). No community has ever provided all the care that its population might be willing to use. The magnitude of consumption has reflected the manpower and facilities available, the price of services, and the noneconomic barriers to care such as queues, waiting time, and distance to sites of care. An important change in recent years, however, is the extent to which services are free of cost to the recipient at the point of consumption. As government and third parties cover an increasing proportion of medical-care costs, there are fewer financial inhibitions on the use of services. Thus the marketplace as a rationing process must be replaced by consciously planned means of rationing either

10

by government edict or through incentives or controls intended to change the behavior of health professionals.

Rationing is simply a means to apportion or distribute some good through a method of allowance. As the marketplace becomes a less important method of allowance, the mix of cost-containment techniques changes. The agenda is to understand better what a good mix is, not only from the perspective of achieving economies, but also to improve quality, enhance interactions between health professionals and patients, and to provide opportunities for trust and mutual respect. More stringent rationing must also be weighed against alternative strategies that either change the dependence of the population on the physician and its demands for more medical care, that improve the production of medical services, or that develop alternative community structures to deal with many types of problems typically treated by physicians.

Factors Affecting the Consumption of Services

A major way to reduce expenditures for medical care and the requirement for developing more facilities and personnel is to limit the needs and desires among patients for medical care. Reducing needs involves the prevention of illness or diminishing patients' psychological dependence on the medical encounter for social support or other secondary advantages. Reducing desire for services requires changing people's views of the value of different types of medical care, making them more aware of the real costs of service in relation to the benefits received, and legitimizing alternatives for dealing with many problems that physicians increasingly deal with as the boundaries of medical care expand.

Prevention can be conceived of broadly as having three aspects. At the most global level are efforts in sectors other than health affecting the quality of the environment, standards of living, education and nutrition, employment, and other social conditions relevant to health status (McKeown 1976). The benefits of pollution control, for example, in relation to cost are high, and such efforts add to health status by reducing prevalence of disease as well as adding to the quality of living (Lave and Seskin 1970). Possibilities for preventive efforts outside the medical sector are considerable, but the required policies frequently compete with economic and other social priorities and may be difficult to implement.

A second approach to prevention involves clearly identifying risk factors and structuring the environment or motivating people to minimize them. Although the examples of cigarette smoking, alcohol and drug dependence, and inactivity and obesity are most frequently cited, these are complex behavioral problems that do not yield simply to exhortation or educational approaches. Often these behaviors are deeply rooted in personality and are related to other serious problems that are intractable to change. There is no reason to be excessively pessimistic about changing the population's habits, since there has been some progress (Farquhar et al. 1977), but it is prudent to recognize the difficulty of the task, the forces working against change, and the depths of ignorance concerning the origins of these behaviors and the ways in which they can best be modified. It may be that the greatest potential in changing health behavior lies in focusing on the young before these behavioral patterns become well entrenched, but overcoming the influence of peer groups and other incentives to dangerous habits remains a formidable task.

A complementary approach is to make efforts to design living environments that reduce risk regardless of individual behavior (Robertson 1975). The inflatable air bag in automobiles, fortified food, and the safe cigarette are examples. Moreover, daily routine patterns of healthful behavior such as exercise (Haggerty 1977) can be introduced into social environments in which persons spend much of their time, such as the work place. Although technological alternatives to changing individual behavior have been vigorously advocated, a prudent social policy would direct efforts to both behavior change and technological alternatives. Too great an emphasis on technology alone might create disincentives for young people to develop responsible behavior relevant to their health.

Closest to the delivery of medical services are primary prevention programs such as immunization and early screening and treatment of disease and disabilities. In such areas as control of hypertension, effective diagnosis and treatment are available, but overcoming the behavioral problem of achieving continuing cooperation still constitutes a major barrier. Early detection of vision and hearing difficulties also limits later problems and costs and does not involve major behavioral barriers. Appropriate treatment of common childhood ailments such as streptococcal infections and otitis media avoids damaging secondary problems that may result in the consumption of considerable services in adult life (Institute of Medicine 1973). The difficulty is that beyond a limited number of instances, preventive or early care remains an untested concept, and the costs of identifying a small number of cases of asymptomatic illness early may be prohibitive (McKeown 1968). To the extent that nontreatable asymptomatic disease is detected and made known to the patient, the consequences may be counterproductive because of the anxiety and worry aroused, socially induced disability, or stigmatization.

Another way of reducing demand for care is to modify patients' perceptions of its value or appropriateness. There seems to be a consensus that patients have exceptionally high and unrealistic expectations of physicians and that they become too dependent on medical care. A number of studies have found that unrealistic expectations result in disappointment and less successful outcomes (Ley and Spelman 1967). Although the medical profession may have contributed to such excessive expectations by exaggerating the effects of medical advances, it is in the interests of both patients and physicians to have the public better informed about the limitations of medical care as well as its benefits. The challenge is to educate the patient without encouraging further distrust of physicians and their work.

Changing expectations is an exercise in modifying the culture of medical care. This process requires changing perceptions of how particular health and illness incidents are to be handled, and such modified conceptions may involve as much adjustment for the physician as for the patient. Extreme examples are the redefinition of the appropriate way to die and the development of hospices, with many preferring a less frantic end in the company of their loved ones and sympathetic health personnel to the stupor and high technology of the intensive-care unit. The growth of technology has shaped services to a larger degree than patients' needs or desires or prudent expenditure patterns would justify. Third-party payment has made it possible to finance new technology without tough consideration of whether its benefits outweigh its costs. Cultural redefinitions would encourage patients to demand different ways of dealing with many problems.

As patients become better educated about the value, but also about the risks and limitations, of many medical procedures, they may be less likely to demand dangerous interventions that are unnecessary. Mothers may become less enthusiastic about tonsillectomies and routine X-ray studies; and patients with ordinary colds, weight problems, and insomnia less demanding of antibiotics, amphetamines, and barbiturates. Moreover, as patients become better informed, less-responsible physicians will have greater difficulties in carrying out inappropriate procedures and treatments. The task is fairly subtle, and the challenge is to teach patients to question constructively and physicians to respond to such questioning appropriately and in a manner that builds on the patient's trust in the physician's competence and good intentions.

Factors Affecting the Production of Services

In recent years there has been increased attention to the training of physician assistants and nurse practitioners, to the development of health-maintenance organizations, and to improved information systems and managerial practices. These may all be ways to increase efficiency in the production of services. Medical care in Western countries is dependent on advanced technologies and expensive personnel. The ordinary medical encounter depends less and less on communication and clinical judgment and increasingly more on a battery of expensive diagnostic procedures and laboratory tests. The bias in medical care is toward what Fuchs has called the technologic imperative (Fuchs 1968)—a tendency to take action, whatever the cost, if it offers even a slight possibility of utility. This situation increases the costs of medical care without evidence that the benefits exceed those of adopting a modest approach.

Methods of production refer to the way in which problems are handled, the time devoted to each case, the routine procedures performed, and the apportionment of tasks among personnel. For example, one Kaiser plan provides a multiphasic health examination performed largely by technicians as a substitute for the more traditional annual examination performed almost exclusively by physicians. Also, clinicians and clinics may vary in the amount of time that they schedule for new and routine visits, the procedures conventionally performed with new patients, and modes of dealing with routine problems. Production of services may be affected in four ways: by changing the mix of personnel involved; by changing the technological inputs; by changing the content of the encounter; or by changing the auspices of care. For example, nurse practitioners can substitute for physicians quite successfully for certain types of care, as a variety of studies have demonstrated (Rabin and Spector 1977), and many aspects of care can be transferred to nurses, physician assistants, and others in a way that improves the productivity of the physician (Reinhardt 1975). Similarly, specialists and subspecialists in primary-care settings order more procedures than family physicians and general practitioners and have longer encounters (Mechanic 1972b). Although such production methods may involve higher quality, the benefits derived from a more intensive technical approach in ambulatory settings remain conjectural (Beeson 1974). The use of laboratory and many other diagnostic and technical aids can be contained not only to reduce cost and limit iatrogenic diseases but also to improve the quality of care (Brook and Williams 1976).

Shifting the auspices of care may involve considerable economies as well. Experience suggests that providing hospital-based ambulatory care often results in more procedures ordered and higher costs. The easy accessibility of X-ray and laboratory facilities encourages discretionary use, and the high proportion of specialists in hospitals may create a climate supporting a high dependence on technical facilities. Gerald Perkoff and associates (1976), in an experiment comparing a hospital-based prepaid practice with more traditional care in the community, found much higher use of X-rays and laboratory services in the hospital-based ambulatory setting. Moreover, studies in relation to a wide variety of conditions suggest that length of stay can be reduced without any demonstrable medical consequences. The wide fluctuations in use of hospital facilities from one area to another, with little difference in morbidity or mortality experiences, suggest that the decision to keep a patient in a hospital is as much a matter of culture as of medical need.

There is a compelling need for investigation of the relationship between production methods and patient outcome. Although there is an implicit bias in medical practice that more is better, alternative production methods that devote time to knowing the patient and communicating effectively may yield more valuable results than increasing the intensity of technology. When the "art of medicine" and social care are considered, the role of functional alternatives becomes more obvious.

Functional Alternatives to Existing Medical-Care Patterns

Developments in medical technology, unless of a preventive type, such as immunization, tend to increase the costs of a typical medical encounter. As more is known and as more can be done, patients' expectations increase, and they demand increased coverage for medical care. To facilitate the effective use of physician resources, it is desirable to shift to other sectors, to the extent possible, those services that nonprofessionals and other types of professionals can provide as well and at less cost.

Although estimates vary depending on the criteria used, there is agreement from both clinical judgments and the epidemiological evidence that much of the demand for medical care arises from conditions that physicians are powerless to change or that are simple in terms of the kinds of care required (White, Williams, and Greenberg 1961). The utilization of medical care is influenced by illness behavior (Mechanic 1978a: 249- 89)—the varied ways in which persons identify, define, and evaluate symptoms and what to do about them. Three modes of illness behavior are most relevant here.

First are the many patients with common self-limited problems that may cause discomfort for a short time but little harm, and that in any case are not amenable to effective medical intervention.

Second is the large variety of minor complaints that can be treated successfully but in which self-care can serve as a suitable substitute with modest self-care aids.

Third, and most problematic, are the relatively large numbers of patients with mild and moderate depressions, anxiety, psychosomatic discomforts, and insomnia who frequently come to physicians seeking relief of distress, support, and reassurance. Epidemiological surveys suggest that at any given time approximately one-fifth of the population may be characterized in this way. Those that come to physicians may be truly suffering, but the hurried and technical stance of the physician in busy ambulatory settings may contribute little to providing the support and comfort that these patients require. The problem of care is made even more difficult because these patients do not explicitly acknowledge the nature of their discomforts, mask these problems with presentations of vague physical symptoms, and often resist psychological redefinitions of their distress (Mechanic 1972c).

Although physicians must continue to deal with many of these problems and must do so more capably, alternatives exist through development of self-help groups, improved community networks of social support, and a variety of voluntary and professional counseling and information services. To the extent that such services are developed, are defined as legitimate, and avoid excessive professionalization of personnel, they are likely to reach more people at lower cost

in relation to benefits, or they can specify when such procedures can be performed or by whom through requirements for review of specific procedures prior to their performance or by specification of necessary credentials for eligibility for reimbursement. Although planned rationing seems like a reasonable approach, it is highly susceptible to public pressures and political influence and does not necessarily result in a fairer allocation of resources (Cooper 1975). And although, in theory, allocation decisions made on an aggregate base are probably better than individual clinical judgments, data in most clinical areas are not sufficiently firm to justify detailed explicit control, and there is the further danger that those who develop guidelines and regulations become too far removed from the complex uncertainties and contingencies of practice, from the large variability that is evident among patients, and from the kind of sensitivity that comes from working with clinical problems.

It has been argued that asking physicians to ration services is to violate their primary responsibility to the patient to do everything possible (Fried 1975). But the ethic of doing everything possible is increasingly unrealistic in the face of biomedical advances (Mechanic 1976d). Explicit rationing is one alternative to physician rationing in that it shifts much of the responsibility for limiting services from the physician to an impersonal third party. Explicit rationing may thus reduce potential conflicts between patients and doctors; it does, however, have serious disadvantages for both: It may seriously limit the physician's professional discretion and the opportunity to respond creatively to unique aspects of the clinical situation. And it removes responsibility for the patient to a more distant authority, one that will be more impervious to appeal or to persuasion.

In the foreseeable future any system of national health insurance introduced will be a mix of rationing by consumer cost sharing and by implicit and explicit methods. There is relatively little firm knowledge about the effects of different methods of rationing on patients, physicians, and the types of relations that evolve between them, and this is a serious question for the near future. The goal is to find a mix of techniques that are responsive to patient need, that enhance the best aspects of physician discretion and clinical judgment, and that protect the public purse.

The choices are not easy, and any serious system of rationing will impose hardships on some. The United States is a wealthy country and is capable of providing a very high level of care. To the extent that opportunities to improve the production of services, and to affect consumer need and desire for them, are taken seriously, they will relieve some of the pressures for more forceful rationing in the future. If rationing is repugnant to health professionals, then they must do what they can to contribute to progress on these other fronts.

II

Patients' Health
Behavior and the
Medical Marketplace

3 | Changing Individual Health Behavior: Rhetoric and Reality

The value of promoting effective health behavior and teaching people to use medical services wisely is undeniable. Such efforts, if successful, not only contribute to improved health and vitality but also diminish the necessity to consume medical-care resources. Efforts in health education, however, have been disappointing. While many risks to health are widely appreciated by the population, such awareness of possible harm is only one of many conditions necessary to achieve more healthful patterns of living. Health education has been primarily concerned with information dissemination and, thus, its limitations have been inevitable. Moreover, the field of health education lacks effective models of behavior acquisition, rarely makes use of existing knowledge of behavior change, and has only begun to examine seriously the implications of its own practice (Richards 1975).

A new ideology is increasingly advanced extolling the importance of individual responsibility for health outcomes (Knowles 1977a; Illich 1976; Fuchs 1974). Such advocacy varies from harmless self-evident declarations that individual lifestyles are linked to health and disease to extreme statements of individual determinism. To quote John Knowles (1977a:78), man's primary critical choice is "to change his personal and bad habits or stop complaining. He can either remain the problem or become the solution to it; Beneficent Government cannot—indeed, should not—do it for him or to him."

The public discussion of the issue of health education abounds in exaggeration, oversimplification, and advocacy of a naive free-will philosophy that seems oblivious to the complexity of behavior and the sociocultural and environmental constraints on it. As Crawford

25

(1977) has observed, it is no accident that this type of blaming of victims emerges during a period when the mounting costs of medical care confront industry, labor, and government with serious problems in collective bargaining and the financing of social programs. Focusing on individual responsibility relieves some of the pressure to increase access to care, to ensure more comprehensive services to the poor, and to deal with the industrial, environmental, and social conditions that pose significant risks to health.

It is too simple, however, to dismiss the concern with health behavior as an ideological diversion. While efforts to change such behavior may offer less promising prospects than technological interventions, economic and environmental modifications, and industrial changes, they are likely to confront fewer barriers and receive more public support than other approaches. There is much that can be achieved even within existing constraints if we conceptualize the problem carefully and use available opportunities to improve our understanding and practices. This chapter examines some possible points of leverage and makes an initial attempt to offer a concept of intervention that may be useful in future health-education efforts. It also speculates on some of the origins of health and illness behavior, suggesting areas of needed research.

There have been signs that the increased focus on health behavior has not been without some impact. The proportion of smokers is lower than might have been expected (Warner 1977), although there is an alarming increase in smoking among teenage girls (U.S. DHEW 1977:17). There are indications of changes in patterns of exercise and of developing interest in nutrition, stress reduction, and emotional growth. Despite many past failures, there is promising evidence that a mass-media approach to modifying major health habits may be possible (Farquhar et al. 1977), and there are signs of increased interest in health-related matters. It is not clear to what extent the progress noted reflects more successful health-education approaches and to what extent it reflects changing age cohorts and economic and sociocultural change. Unfortunately, new risks to health in the environment and in industry seem to arise faster than we can monitor, and progress achieved may be rapidly overtaken by new health threats.

Although the encouragement of effective health behavior as part of a national health strategy is widely discussed, there has been relatively little serious effort to conceptualize what is really involved in designing programs, instituting social change, or defining needed research to inform such efforts. There has been advocacy of using the tax or insurance structure to penalize persons with poor health behavior, but these are generally superficial discussions that fail to examine the social, behavioral, or ethical implications of such recommendations. They are based on a combination of naive free-will ideology and vulgar behaviorism and ignore the fact that "poor health habits" are complex patterns of behavior deeply entrenched in human personality with biological, developmental, and sociocultural antecedents that we do not really understand.

Unreliability of Health-Promotion Information

Health education is likely to be most effective when the relevant audience desires it, needs it, and is ready to act upon it. While providing appropriate information seems like a modest goal, there are innumerable barriers to it. The population is constantly bombarded with health advice dealing with almost every aspect of their behavior. Such advice is motivated to sell commercial products, to encourage behavior consistent with certain moral norms, or to provide expert advice consistent with healthful behavior change. Even the expert advice, however, is characterized by disagreements and inconsistencies because the fields involved are uncertain. The average informed person has difficulty ascertaining whether taking vitamin C and other substances is advantageous to health, whether jogging is helpful or harmful for the heart, whether diets high in cholesterol truly increase risk of myocardial infarction, and whether persons with past alcohol difficulties can drink again. Indeed, beyond the gratuitous advice to pursue moderation, to avoid smoking, unnecessary drugs, and excessive alcohol, and to have some exercise, much of the remainder of the content called health education seeks to promote behaviors about which the experts themselves disagree. In many areas advice goes in cycles, as in such cases as proper brushing of teeth or weight gain during pregnancy. Even if the providers of information wanted to present a united front, it is evident that they could not. The more persistent seeker of information, thus, finds that the greater the depth of his inquiry, the less he seems to know about what is good for him.

A host of experts, for example, extol the virtue of exercise for physical fitness. Although some encourage moderate exercise with admonitions to avoid too strenuous an activity, others encourage primarily strenuous exercise. While many encourage jogging, two reputably eminent cardiologists tell us in a widely promoted book that "first on our blacklist is jogging. This miserable postcollegiate athletic travesty has already killed at least scores, possibly hundreds of Americans" (Friedman and Rosenman 1974:158). They then go on to bring into question, at least for those over thirty-five, "competitive handball, tennis singles, and squash." When the hucksters are added to the equation, the situation becomes even more problematic. Lewis and Lewis (1974), in examining commercial health measures on television, found that the vast majority were believed by young children. Adults become more skeptical, especially of efforts they see as motivated to change their behavior, but they may be more influenced inadvertently by general media programming. Such programming, whatever else one might say about it, is not particularly oriented toward health promotion.

Conflicting Goals and Needs

It is a truism, but also an essential fact, that actions that promote health often come into conflict with other social goals and personal needs. With the growing energy crisis, for example, consumers are encouraged to purchase smaller cars that consume less gas. The size and weight of the car, however, are added protection in case of collision, and serious injuries are much more likely to occur in smaller vehicles. Similarly, social arrangements and recreation patterns encourage not only the consumption of alcohol but also consumption in settings other than the home, which increases the probability of drunken driving. We encourage persons to reduce stress and harassments in their lives, but our emphasis on competition, professional success, and material acquisition betrays our lack of seriousness.

The conflict in goals at the individual level is reflected at larger policy levels. While one agency of the federal government encourages reduction in smoking, others subsidize tobacco farming and cigarette smoking overseas. Inaction in reducing environmental risks or industrial hazards is commonplace because of the economic costs and relocations required to achieve these goals. The control of hazardous drugs must be balanced against the danger of discouraging innovation in development or in delaying the use of new effective drugs. And so on.

Contextual Demands on Behavior

Much of our behavior, whether health-relevant or not, arises from a long period of socialization and from the contextual demands of the environments in which we work and play. Good or bad health practices are most typically integrated into our daily routines, our patterns of work or family life, and social demands and expectations. If our work requires us to remain active, we are much more likely to do so than if we must make a conscious decision. To the extent that healthful patterns of behavior are programmed into our daily routines, they are more likely to be practical than if they require continuing conscious efforts. A variety of studies suggest higher levels of health status and lower prevalence of particular diseases among such groups as Mormons and Seventh-Day Adventists (Mechanic 1978a:58, 212). These groups may be no more health-conscious than others, but the patterns of culture that shape their behaviors are more likely to be conducive to the protection of health. Changing patterns of health behavior, thus, involves reshaping cultural assumptions and reinforcements—clearly a major task.

Healthful behavior, whatever its components, is more likely to occur if reinforced by supportive groups, peer pressures, media, and other community influences (Haggerty 1977). To the extent that healthful behavior can successfully be buttressed by community regulation, as in growing restrictions on smoking in public places, useful constraints are set on harmful behaviors. The regulation of smoking is an instructive example in illustrating the way relatively mild forms of social regulation assisted in reversing the definition of the social situation. While previously nonsmokers were on the defensive, increasingly the social support available through regulation allows them to be more assertive in insisting on their own needs and wishes. Smokers are now more apologetic about smoking in public places, and growing environmental constraints may be affecting the rate at which they smoke. How to develop social constraints affecting harmful behaviors without inflicting undue pain on individuals who cannot help themselves or without seriously interfering with their right to choose their own lifestyle is an important issue.

It is useful to distinguish between unhealthy behavior that harms and inconveniences others, such as smoking, drunk driving, and public drunkenness, and forms of behavior primarily harmful to the person involved, such as drug taking, obesity, and inactivity. In principle it is more justifiable to impose constraints in the former instances because such behaviors infringe significantly on the rights and welfare of others. But even in such cases as public drunkenness, imposing greater constraints may be contrary to a satisfactory rehabilitative attitude or community standards of appropriateness. In recent years we have significantly loosened such constraints by decriminalizing alcoholism, and societal trends in general are in the direction of reducing constraints, particularly in those areas of behavior in which no unwilling victims are involved.

For the most part we are dealing with patterns of behavior that individuals have difficulty controlling. Experience with obese persons suggests how difficult it is to achieve weight reduction on any long-term basis and how agonizing the process often is (Stunkard 1976). Similarly, smoking, excessive drinking, drug taking, and a variety of other behaviors potentially harmful to health are often means people use to deal with disillusionments, anxieties, and other life stresses. Thus the new rhetoric of self-reliance is deceptive and masks a highly moralistic stance to deep human dilemmas. Like the notion that nations would not be at war if they would only cooperate, the new health moralism seems to have more to say than it really does.

Behavior Models in Health Education

The health-belief model has probably had more influence on health education efforts than any other. This model has implied a motivational theory that behavior emerges from conflicting goals and motives and reflects those that are most important and most salient (Rosenstock 1960). The implicit cognitive calculus involves the person's evaluation of the consequences of a particular problem and its probability of occurrence as well as the benefits and costs of pursuing a particular course of action. Most health-education programs attempt to influence the way the individual calculates the risks of an illness, the probability that he or she is vulnerable, and the benefits of taking recommended actions. Proponents of the health-belief model have found, however, that whatever the cognitive calculus, additional forces are necessary to trigger the healthful activity. They thus give considerable attention to cues to action that are necessary for the initiation of a behavioral sequence (Rosenstock 1969). The cue may be an interpersonal contact, knowledge about the immediate availability of preventive services, or information that a well-known person or a relative has developed the disease in question.

Despite the intuitive attractiveness of the health-belief model as an organizing perspective and as a research paradigm, it has had only modest success in predicting health behavior (Rosenstock 1969). When the variables in the model are interpreted broadly, it applies to a wider range of situations (Becker 1974), but it still leaves a great deal unexplained. The model in emphasizing psychological rationality and motivational factors gives too little attention to the irrational aspects of behavior and to coping, and these shortcomings may account in part for its modest success.

One way of conceptualizing the task of the health educator is as a programmer of thinking and behavioral processes. Individuals faced with changes in their physical or psychological responses usually go through a process of hypothesis testing in which they attempt to make sense of what they are experiencing, the meaning of what is happening, and the likely causes. This intuitive process has potential dangers because it may result in little attention to changes that are not particularly disruptive to functioning even though the symptoms may be medically serious or it may unduly delay the help-seeking process. What the health educator attempts to do is substitute a more functional behavioral program for the intuitive appraisal and decision-making process the individual experiences.

Consider, for example, the media campaign to identify early signs of cancer. Typically, the public is appraised of the most common signs of cancer, such as continued bleeding, lump in a breast, or growth of a mole, and told to consult a physician immediately when this symptom occurs. This might be seen as substituting an immediate help-seeking instruction for the usual search-and-appraisal process that takes place when a person first becomes aware of symptoms. Because the original programming of the person has some probability of delay or neglect, the health educator wishes to short-circuit the usual psychological process with a clear behavioral instruction.

Health action requires an awareness of a problem, a willingness to do something about it, and a capacity to execute the necessary behavior. Educators, thus, must not only alert persons to a potential problem, but must ensure that they see some urgency in taking action and know what to do. One means of inducing willingness is by achieving some degree of anxiety or fear. Although early experimental evidence was interpreted to suggest that excessive levels of fear resulted in denial (Janis and Feshbach 1953), more recent data suggest that this occurs primarily when the person has no way to cope. When there is an apparent coping strategy, a high level of fear is an inducement to action (Leventhal 1970). Educators must be careful, however, in depending on fear as a motivator, because it frequently results in the constriction of the individual's identification of alternatives and may lead to a poor coping strategy (Janis and Mann 1977). In short, inducing high fear may be effective when the desired action is known and easily executed but may be counterproductive in situations in which appropriate solutions are uncertain.

One aspect central to health action, but often neglected by educators, is the implementation of health behavior. There is much inertia in initiating behavior outside of usual routines, and persons must not only become aware that action is necessary but also know how to perform the necessary behavior. Such behavior may be facilitated by developing a clear plan of action and showing the person how it can be executed within usual routines (Leventhal 1970). This may involve not only information as to the fact that a helper is available but also instruction on how to get there, how to schedule an appointment, and the like. Or if the behavior involves exercise or nutrition, it is not enough to indicate the types of action necessary; one must also specify how to schedule and perform them within the context of everyday routines.

Like with coping efforts more generally, appropriate health behavior has societal as well as personal aspects (Mechanic 1974b). Awareness of health risks and necessary health action is dependent on the adequacy of social programming in the family, the schools, and the mass media. Incidental learning within the context of other activities may be more important than those activities formally designated as "health education." Also, the willingness of individuals to take appropriate health actions depends on the social incentives and rewards for such behavior. Much poor health behavior in our society is rewarded both purposefully and inadvertently. In the long run, we have to build more incentives and social support for positive and promotive health behavior. To the extent that it is "cool" to be physically fit, avoid smoking, drive carefully, and wear seat belts, more people are likely to do so. At the same time that we initiate behavior change at the individual level, we must make efforts to use potentialities at the structural level to make possible and reinforce individual actions.

Implicit in much of the thinking about health education is an assumption of some underlying syndrome of healthful behavior. All evidence to date, however, suggests that there is considerable individual variability in behavior from one health-relevant area to another (Williams and Wechsler 1972; Steele and McBroom 1972), and that it is more productive to focus on each item of behavior we wish to change than to think in terms of a global health orientation. Although "staying healthy" may be a general value, each component of behavior is partly a product of incentives for and against it and reinforcements in the environment. Behaviors promoting health are most likely to be performed when they are rewarding on their own terms and not when they are performed specifically to avoid some future negative outcome.

The Development of Health and Illness Behavior

There are a variety of psychological theories that attempt to account for the origins and persistence of behavior. Relevant factors include constitutional influences, early imprinting, social reinforcement in the family or in other culturally established settings, and modeling. Although some patterns of psychological response are shaped fairly early in life, many habits relevant to improving health do not become issues until adolescence or early adulthood. Such behavioral patterns as smoking, drinking, or drug use, although they may have constitutional or early-childhood antecedents, do not usually become evident until the adolescent becomes involved in peer groups.

Most young children are healthy, and the average child has only routine contacts with medical care. Thus the healthy child learns much of what he or she knows about illness inadvertently, while the child with more illness may learn more directly. Knowledge of how healthy children differ in their concepts of illness and medical care as contrasted with children with some chronic illness who have had considerable direct contact with medical services would be valuable. In the latter case one might expect the child to have a more specified and complex view of illness and to be more conscious and sensitive to symptoms.

Much of what the child learns depends on reactions of the parents and the modeling that takes place in the family. Parents may be more or less protective and may caution their children about risky behavior, diet, and avoidance of a variety of alleged risks to health. Parents also may be more or less responsive to the child's complaints of illness. Children may learn that pleading sickness has a variety of secondary benefits or that it will be discouraged, frowned upon, or even ridiculed.

One aspect of behavior that appears to be learned fairly early is the somatization of psychological distress. Children learn at a very early age that complaints of stomachaches or headaches often result in a solicitous response from the parent or teacher and a release from expected behaviors. It is not clear whether such childhood complaints are common in response to stress because children have difficulty in conceptualizing their feelings or simply because they learn that such complaints have their intended effect. In any case, the somatization of distress becomes a difficult problem for the medical-care system to handle and contributes significantly to excessive use of medical interventions. Self-esteem is an important facet of effective health behavior, and the way children view themselves and their efficacy to affect their own lives and their own decisions is crucial to their health and well-being.

Because health, illness, and medical care are not of prime interest among youth peer groups, early learning acquired in the family is rarely discussed or reviewed against the experience of others. Such learning thus tends to be a relatively private issue that is not validated through continuing testing. Adolescents are subjected, of course, to information on health and illness through magazines, school, television, and the like, but their conceptions of their own bodies and the medical process are not as subject to influences outside the home as sexual patterns, drinking and drug use, recreational interests, and driving.

When facing a problem with illness, young adults have no well-defined sick role or repertoire for dealing with the medical-care system. It is at such times that they may draw on the patterns of response that were programmed in earlier periods. Such reactions as stoicism or complaining, degree of dependency on physicians, trust or skepticism of physicians, persisting with usual roles or seeking relief—these and many other aspects of response probably depend on early socialization, parental values and behavior, and experience in the family. We have no clear idea, however, as to the transmission process. What is clear is that there is no one-to-one correspondence between parental behavior and child response (Mechanic 1964). Moreover, the child's parents have different modes of dealing with illness, and even the same parent may vary in response from one time to another. Also, parents differ in the ways they respond to their own illnesses and those of their children, and we have no idea which of these responses have greater impact on the child. Finally, parents and the community at large have different expectations of boys and girls, and thus socialization is likely to reflect this, accounting in part for the substantial differences in health and illness behavior between men and women (Mechanic 1976b; Lewis and Lewis 1977).

Certainly there are important variables that intervene between the parental response and socialization outcomes. The child develops opinions about the illness behavior he sees in the family, and he may strive to develop quite different patterns of behavior than those that characterize the parental response. The degree of modeling may depend on the identification of the child with the parent at the critical times, the warmth of the parent toward the child, and other variables of this kind.

During the teenage years children assert their independence of parents and often seem oblivious to threats and risks parents seem concerned about. During this phase the inattention of the teenager to diet, sleep, weather, or other alleged risks to health gives the illusion that attempts to teach prudence in health matters were of no avail. This is a developmental period in which the child typically asserts independence of the family, and health is not a particularly salient issue. While the teenager will have the usual self-limited acute conditions, the prevalence of serious illness during this period is very low, and the teenager rarely confronts the medical-care system except for routine types of care.

It is during late adolescence that the child may leave the home to attend college or work and that greater responsibility for one's own health may be achieved. Because children have had limited contacts with the medical-care system and have not exercised full responsibility for their own health, expectations of the system may be uninformed and unrealistic. It is during the college years that data begin to become available on health and illness behavior, in large part because college students are excellent "captive" respondents. One striking aspect of the perceptions of college students about health care is their almost universal criticism of student health services at universities and their ambivalence about physicians. On the one hand they frequently have extremely high expectations of doctors, while on the other they are bitterly critical of physician behavior and inconveniences in obtaining services that the community population more readily accepts. This ambivalence may be a product of the fact that young people have learned idealized conceptions of physicians typical of the mass media but only begin to test these cultural images during the college years. Although most student health services at large universities offer medical services comparable in quality and amenities to those available in the larger community, students tend frequently to regard these services with low esteem, and atrocity stories of incompetence and bad medical care are widely shared. When attempts are made to trace these stories to their source, which I have tried to do from time to time, it is difficult to do so. As the story usually goes, "It happened to a friend of a friend."

We know little about the continuity of health and illness behavior. Continuity is itself a complex concept (Kagan 1976) and may refer to the retention of one's rank over time in a defined cohort, or the manifestation of the same behavioral response over time, or the linkage between earlier responses and different but related adult patterns. Although there is some evidence that such dispositions as aggressiveness, passivity, and dependence may have considerable stability from early to later life, we know almost nothing about the continuity of most health-behavior responses. Some patterns seem to emerge fairly early in life, structured by routines developed in the family. Others seem to become most problematic during adolescence, when young people are influenced more by peer groups and the media. Still others develop as the young adult establishes regularity in living patterns with the assumption of adult occupational and family roles. Early socialization in the family may establish basic patterns from which there may be a great deal of deviation during the unsettling period of adolescence but which may serve as a framework for later adult response patterns. This discussion should make clear that we know extraordinarily little about how the patterns of behavior implicit in the concern for "individual responsibility for health" are formed and sustained. Nor are we clear about how they can be modified despite the frequent calls to action. The research agenda remains very large.

A Note on Structural Barriers to Individual Responsibility

In focusing on what individuals can and should do for themselves, there is the danger of neglecting structural barriers. The
medical-care system itself does a great deal to foster dependence and
to inhibit self-care. For example, one of the most prevalent conditions among children is sore throats, and it is routine to take a throat
culture before treatment to assess whether the cause is a streptococcal infection. Typically, the mother is required to bring the child to a
pediatrician for the culture, often involving inconvenience and considerable expense. As an experiment at the Columbia Medical Plan
has demonstrated, mothers can be effectively instructed to take a
throat culture at home, negating the need for physician and nurse
care in most instances and increasing the convenience and satisfaction of the mother (Katz and Clancy 1974). The barriers to individual responsibility *built in to* medical care must be reviewed
carefully, and efforts should be made to modify them. Because such
dependence is remunerative for physicians, it will not be changed
easily.

Health education, thus, is an area of potential but one that must
recognize its limited tools and uncertain knowledge of basic behavioral processes. Rather than allying itself with the new "cult of
individual responsibility," it would do well to develop further its
strategies of change, seek to acquire more basic understanding of
behavior modification, and critically evaluate its own practices and
performance. Similarly, the policymaker ought not to be taken in by
vacuous claims and superficial approaches simply because they pur-
port to teach responsibility for health. The problem is deeper and
more difficult than the public discussion suggests, and in the long run
progress will depend on learning a great deal more about the way
patterns of health and health behavior develop, are sustained, and
can be modified. Although there is a great deal we can do now to
inform the public better and to facilitate desired actions among those
who wish to change their behavior, we largely lack the knowledge,
technology, and political control to alter our patterns of culture, but
this is precisely what health education must eventually do.

4 | Making the Medical Marketplace Work: Psychological Considerations

A major difference between marketplace advocates and those supporting regulatory approaches is their assumptions about the ability of consumers to make informed choices. While economists tend to have an implicit faith in the integrity of consumer choice, those who support planning models tend to see consumers as victims of an elaborate bureaucratic web that makes it difficult for even well-educated and sophisticated clients to make prudent decisions. Thus while market advocates support greater pluralism, consumer cost sharing, and limited regulation, the planning approach focuses on designing systems of care for defined population areas that depend more on expert assessment than on consumer preferences among competing alternatives.

Because both views tend to arise from strong ideological commitments, neither camp is swayed easily in its assumptions. Neither readily acknowledges the extent to which consumers and professionals vary in their personalities, tastes, knowledge, experience, and competence to make informed judgments. Although major proposals for national health insurance arise from these diverse theoretical approaches, advocates of neither seem to be particularly receptive to evidence or analysis that questions the assumptive worlds from which they proceed.

There is widespread recognition that the medical marketplace deviates markedly from competitive assumptions and that few markets for products or services have so many distinctive noncompetitive features (Klarman 1965; Arrow 1963; Mechanic 1978b). Yet, as we consider approaches to national health insurance, the notion of a "fair market test" is dominant in much of the discussion (Havighurst

1973; 1977). Many economists and government officials, as well as much of the public at large, believe in the value of consumer cost sharing as a means of inducing informed choice and greater efficiencies in the distribution and consumption of health-care services. While it is conceded that the medical marketplace has serious imperfections, it is assumed that some modifications—such as the introduction of advertising and better information, fewer restrictions on competing types of health personnel, and encouragement of price competition—would provide increased vigor to the marketplace as an effective means of allocation. This concept is inherent in much of the thinking about national health insurance, and an important proposal by Alain Enthoven, the Consumer Choice Health Plan, is built on the assumption that "the private market needs to be restructured, and that a reconstituted private market can do a better job than a government monopoly of health insurance" (Enthoven 1977:20; 1978a; 1978b).

Advocates of the private marketplace in medical care give little attention to the conditions necessary to allow persons to make informed choices or to those aspects of medical care in which such choices may be more or less possible. On the assumption that the private market in medical care will remain in some form for the foreseeable future, the task of this chapter will be to address some of the psychological conditions necessary for market advocates to achieve their objectives and some of the likely constraints. There is little doubt that increasing consumer sovereignty can contribute to improved medical care under any system of medical care we introduce, but we cannot achieve this by ignoring the obvious difficulties and barriers.

It is important to differentiate not only among varying capacities of consumers but also among varying types of medical products. Purchasing an insurance policy, buying needed drugs, obtaining eyeglasses, selecting a surgeon for an operation, and having vague but troubling symptoms diagnosed are all somewhat different situations offering varying possibilities for constructive consumer decision making. For convenience, such services can be classified into three discrete groups: the purchase of insurance options, the purchase of discrete services of a more or less standard form, and the purchase of services that are part of a process of medical decision making and medical care. These three types constitute a continuum, with difficulties greatest for consumer decision making when the diagnostic procedure or treatment is part of an uncertain appraisal and decision-

making process. The discussion begins by considering the most difficult aspect, the actual process of medical care. Later, means to
improve consumer choice among health-care plans and discrete services will be reviewed briefly.

The Medical Marketplace and the Process of Medical Care

The concepts of supply and demand as used by economists
embody certain simple assumptions about consumer behavior: that
consumers know what they want, that they can make reasonable
assessments of the effectiveness of various products and services in
attaining these ends, and that they know the price necessary to
obtain the desired service (Reynolds 1976:91-97). Presumably this
information is then used in a cost-benefit calculus in which the
person decides on the mix of products and services that will be
purchased. Economists, of course, use such assumptions as a model
to predict behavior and not necessarily as descriptions of behavior,
but it is assumed that they more or less fit the acquisition of most
products and services. However, they very poorly describe the purchase of professional services, particularly medical care.

Considering the issue of whether consumers of medicine know
what they want, Grossman (1972) is probably correct in his assumption that they most generally wish to purchase health, as exemplified
by a feeling of well-being, an absence of pain, discomfort, and
disability, and the avoidance of premature death. At times they wish
to purchase other outcomes such as an excuse for failing to meet
responsibilities or a justification for compensation (Mechanic
1978a:249-89). Consumers, however, only indirectly achieve their
most basic wants through the purchase of care, because the links
between processes of care and the outcomes desired are unclear.
Most consumers tend to be optimistic about these links, however,
and in any case often obtain reassurance, support, and comfort
through medical encounters.

Objectively, there is an indeterminate link between what the
patient wants and what the physician provides. Because of the large
inequality of information between patient and physician, the patient
must have trust that the processes of care are in the interests of his
goals, and thus trust itself is a central component of the service being
purchased. Once the patient is in the hands of the physician, he must

have faith that the physician will perform the most appropriate procedures, tests, and treatments. At times it might be possible to seek a second opinion or to ignore the physician's recommendations, but in its essentials the process itself must be governed by the physician. Although patients can attempt to test the appropriateness of their care by making comparisons with the alleged behavior of other doctors under seemingly similar circumstances or by the extent to which they feel better, these tests are unreliable and often inappropriate.

Complicating the matter further is the fact that patients may not only lack knowledge of the relationship between what they purchase and health but may also be confused or misguided about what they want from the medical encounter. Patients come to physicians with complaints, and the role of the physician is to identify the underlying basis of the complaint so that it can be managed effectively. If the patient complains, for example, of fever, the role of the physician is not simply to reduce the fever but if possible to identify and treat basic causes. Thus the patient's and the physician's conceptions of the medical-care process may be discrepant, but because the patient accepts the physician's greater knowledge and experience, he usually yields to the doctor's definition of the situation. In addition, the use of medical care is related to complex motivational factors that may mask explicit acknowledgment of what the patient wants, and these needs may be hidden not only to avoid social disapproval but because the problem may be to a substantial degree outside the patient's awareness (Mechanic 1972c). A large literature exists on the way patients present problems to physicians and the underlying psychodynamics of these problems, but economists universally ignore such considerations.

There is considerable literature, for example, indicating that distress is an important trigger in the use of medical care, although patients may present symptoms to physicians that are very common in the general population (Tessler et al. 1976). Frequently the patient comes to the physician complaining of a variety of diffuse complaints but without any clear idea of the nature of the problem. These patients may have difficult social and psychological problems that contribute to the distress they feel but which they do not acknowledge because of prior learning, culturally acquired inhibitions, or whatever. A subtle bargaining process must then take place between physician and patient in which they attempt together to arrive at an acceptable construction of the problem (Balint 1957). If the physician too obviously labels the patient as having a problem that the patient is unprepared to accept, rapport may be lost and the patient may even choose another doctor. Both patients and doctors understand this process at some intuitive level, and this in part explains why free choice of physician is an important idea to both.

Economists have given little attention to markets characterized by such psychological complexity and uncertainty. Although it may be argued that things are never what they may seem and that people purchase televisions, cameras, and cars for many reasons, the analogy is a poor one because in each case the product is distinct from the encounter. But in medical care the product is the encounter.

Professional-client relationships, particularly in medical care, are characterized by great inequality in knowledge. Although physicians can share more information with patients than they now do, and studies indicate that patients prefer more feedback (Ley and Spelman 1967), they cannot within any reasonable period of time provide sufficient information for patients to make informed judgments except in those instances in which the costs and risks involved are very large. Even here, medical practice frequently fails because of the pressures of time, the inability of physicians to communicate options effectively, or the doctor's assumption that the patient cannot really understand.

A further complication is that as the stakes of medical care increase, the patient is more commonly under stress. In such situations persons often find themselves unable to weigh alternatives rationally, and many prefer a practitioner they trust to assume the burden of decision. Indeed, what most patients want is a physician in whom they have confidence at a critical time, one whose judgment and commitment are trustworthy. In periods of high stress in which decisions must be made quickly, persons often reveal a pattern of hypervigilance that is associated with cognitive constriction, perseveration, and disrupted thought processes and that interferes significantly with rational choice (Janis and Mann 1977). Patients want to have major options and risks explained but also to be protected from unnecessary distress and worry. The physician's task is not to conform to some standard mandate, but to judge the patient's wishes, his psychological state and capacities, and the contingencies of the situation, and to relate to the patient in light of these considerations.

Consumers want high-quality medical care, but the measurement of the quality of medical care is extraordinarily difficult (Brook 1974). Ideally, we seek to find evidence linking specific patterns of care to improved outcomes as measured by increased longevity, reduced disability, and enhanced comfort, but such data are limited. Physicians thus typically evaluate quality by determining if logical processes in diagnosis and treatment were followed, whether or not such processes have been actually correlated with improved outcome. Although patients are sensitive to continued discomfort and disability, even the best physician may have limited capacity to reduce their distress. Thus patients commonly judge physicians by formal qualifications, the extent to which the physician correctly predicted the course of the illness, and the degree to which the doctor conforms to expectations. Because it is so difficult to obtain specific information about the physician's competence, most patients assume competence and make their judgments on less central features of the relationship. Judgments tend to be made on the physician's countenance and behavior—whether the physician communicates a personal interest in the patient, whether he listens carefully, whether he shows a sympathetic concern and provides feedback, and whether he appears to know what he is doing. Although these are all important elements of the relationship and worthy of concern, they may not be particularly good predictors of the physician's knowledge or his diagnostic and treatment skills.

Although in a trivial sense patients may know the price of medical care, as in knowing the physician's typical fee, those with serious problems have no way of assessing what an episode of illness is likely to cost or whether going to one doctor or another would have different cost implications. Except for routine situations, even the doctor might have difficulty predicting cost because he cannot know beforehand where his assessment of the patient will take him and what problems he is likely to encounter. Thus the physician is likely to proceed in making costly decisions which the patient usually learns about only when he receives his bill.

Unless the patient is a member of a prepaid medical plan or has a comparable comprehensive insurance program, he is unable to calculate what his medical-care costs will be, either in specific episodes or in the aggregate. Although he can price selected elements of service, such as the cost of an ophthalmological examination, a psychotherapy hour, or a particular drug, he has little control over the way physicians will use diagnostic and laboratory aids or what he will be charged for them. It has been suggested that advertising and fee listings would improve consumer choice. These may be valuable in themselves, but they are unlikely to have much effect except at the margins. Neither really deals with the processes through which most costs are generated, and, in any case, because of patients' typical insecurities and real risks of exploitation, they will not necessarily show preference for those charging the lowest fees.

Finally, when people are seriously ill or suffering extensive discomfort, there is a tendency to see price as irrelevant. The typical response is to urge the physician to do whatever he can to relieve the situation, and physicians tend to proceed in this fashion in any case (Fuchs 1968). Because patients cannot possibly monitor the physician's actions in an effective way, they must have faith in the physician's integrity or in the system of controls within which the physician practices.

Physicians commonly maintain that the organization of the medical community and peer review protect the patient from irrational or rapacious decisions. There is little evidence to support this view, however, and except for surgical work and some limited types of medical care the decisions of individual physicians are not particularly visible to colleagues (Freidson 1970a). Given the uncertainties of medical practice, the bias among physicians to take whatever actions seem possible even when they offer minimal probability of advantage, and the tendency of physicians to protect one another from criticism or embarrassment, it is highly unlikely that corrective efforts would be made except in cases of obvious fraud, malpractice, and incompetence, and even in these areas there are no assurances. As Freidson (1975) has noted, even in a fairly tightly run group-practice situation such review was relatively weak because physicians give great emphasis to individual autonomy and clinical responsibility and reject the legitimacy of administrative authority in clinical areas. If such controls are problematic in highly organized groups, they are far less feasible in independent practice.

Improving Consumer Choice: Problems and Prospects

Although the foregoing discussion suggests that the marketplace cannot function effectively at the level of the individual medical encounter, the prospects are somewhat more promising in respect to selected components of service and in choosing among health-care plans. In these instances the consumer has a clearer idea of what he wishes to purchase, and if appropriate information is available on alternatives, an informed choice becomes possible.

Because patients place high value on their personal physicians and because needs during illness are not particularly salient when people are well, there tends to be considerable inertia among consumers (Tessler and Mechanic 1975; Mechanic and Tessler 1973). To the extent that people have a satisfactory relationship with their physician, they tend to be reluctant to enter any plan that limits the continuation of the relationship even when there are obvious economic benefits in doing so (Donabedian 1965). Yet there are sufficient numbers of people who place less value on the relationship, or who have no such relationship or an unsatisfactory one, who benefit from having options. Moreover, many insurance options need not limit choice of physician, thus providing alternatives even to those patients committed to a particular practitioner, clinic, or hospital.

Insurance options in the private and nonprofit sectors, however, are now so complicated and vary in so many details that even sophisticated consumers have difficulty in making informed choices. One approach would be to require insurers to market coverage in standard modules that allow better comparisons among policies offering different benefits. Both state insurance departments and consumer groups could provide objective analyses of competing policies that assist the purchaser in making choices better suited to his or her needs. Similarly, information could be made available for the pricing of drugs, appliances, eyeglasses, dental services, surgical fees, prenatal and delivery care, and other components of service that can be defined as discrete units. Although quality may remain an issue, consumers have little basis in selecting among licensed professionals, and in any case knowing price may affect choices. For example, a woman selecting an obstetrician may be very much influenced by the personal manner and warmth of the doctor, but fees may not be irrelevant. Even in the case where physician referral is involved, having fees public puts a burden on the referring physician to justify his choice when he selects a physician charging substantially more than the norm. Having fees listed thus is likely to reduce variance.

The Enthoven (1977) proposals as well as others are oriented less toward achieving competition among physicians and more toward inducing competition among sellers of insurance programs. To the extent that such competition is achieved, it is assumed that the plans will increasingly pressure physicians for more efficient behavior in order to obtain a competitive advantage in the marketplace. It is further assumed that under such conditions organizations such as health-maintenance organizations (HMOs) are more likely to emerge because they exercise greater control over the use of expensive resources and can offer more benefits at lower premiums.

At the present time dual-choice situations are less effective than might be possible because of the inertia common among purchasers who feel secure in staying with what they know and what has generally been acceptable in the past. In studies of decision making in dual-choice situations, consumers usually give responses that indicate nominal decision making more than tough comparisons among alternatives. Most consumers, when given a choice between a traditional insurance policy and a new option such as an HMO, will stay with their previous coverage. When asked how they came to make this choice, the majority of the responses indicate that a careful decision was not made. Many will concede that they did not have sufficient information, others will simply say that they were satisfied with what they had, and still others simply report inertia. The most common reason given, if the dual choice involves a closed panel as part of one of the options, is unwillingness to change physicians. If additional cost is involved in choosing a new alternative, such costs are frequently noted as the reason for rejecting the option. Such studies suggest that effective choice situations will require much more information and guidance than has been typical for consumers in making comparisons.

Conclusion

Although the opportunities for introducing informed medical choice in the medical marketplace are greater than critics assume, there are serious psychological obstacles to consumer sovereignty. These obstacles are particularly acute when patients are ill, frightened, and otherwise under stress. The uncertainties of illness and the medical encounter as well as the underlying processes of illness behavior make it difficult to designate the specific objectives, components, and utilities associated with doctor–patient transactions. While economic theory cannot be applied effectively to such encounters, it is more useful for considering the organizational framework within which such encounters take place.

The most advantageous point of application of marketplace assumptions is in the selling of alternative insurance options. However, more information is necessary on alternatives, organized and presented in ways that ordinary consumers or their representatives can understand if existing consumer inertia is to be overcome. The marketing of standard insurance modules would facilitate more effective comparison, allowing consumers realistically to appraise benefits against costs. Information should also be available on various performance and consumer-satisfaction criteria. Data on average time to achieve access to an acute-care appointment, average waiting time, and other indices of availability of services would be helpful.

Although the value of fee schedules and other pricing information is often exaggerated, such information, if readily available, would be useful to consumers in the pricing of discrete services and medical products, such as drugs, eye refractions, eyeglasses, surgical fees, and prenatal care. While at the margins this might make some difference, it is unlikely to have any fundamental or pervasive influence on patterns of medical-care consumption.

The nature of a highly professionalized and technical service such as medical care and the anxieties and uncertainties that surround the management of illness make it very unlikely that effective competition can be introduced at the level of the medical encounter. But if such competition is introduced effectively at the health-plan level, certain competitive constraints may trickle downward to affect the behavior of physicians as well. Thus competition in the medical-insurance marketplace may assist in constraining the most blatant abuses at the patient-care level. It is certainly an approach worth pursuing but not at the exclusion of other efforts in the planning and regulatory fields. An appropriate mix of increased competition, improved planning, and prudent and parsimonious regulation if coordinated may do a great deal to improve the rationality of the organization and delivery of health services.

longitudinal perspective. The latter involves forms of organization outside the medical institution and types of coordination and integration of programs and agencies that require particularly skillful administration (Mechanic 1978c). It also involves larger uncertainties in professional roles, less formal authority to ensure the desired responses because of the range of professionals and agencies involved, and the absence of a clearly defined and understood institutional structure that can be taken for granted by each of the various professionals involved. Traditional patterns of care are embodied in the mind-sets and professional routines of the actors involved. Thus, performing professional tasks and the coordination among personnel are part of an implicit process that has been molded by professional socialization and experience. Developing new patterns of care requires more conscious efforts to compensate for the absence of an appropriate professional culture, and successful implementation requires considerable skill and momentum.

Defining the Goals of Long-Term Care

In dealing with traditional patterns of care, we often take for granted the goals toward which our efforts are directed. Although it is always useful—even in traditional areas—to think carefully about goals, such definitions are particularly essential in areas of care that are outside the mainstream of usual service patterns. In long-term care our therapeutic goals are to maximize the social functioning of patients and to minimize their discomforts and disabilities as much as we can. This involves making whatever efforts are possible to contain disability even when we lack the ability to change in any fundamental way the underlying processes causing it. Social disability can be contained by teaching new skills, providing various types of social supports, and assisting the patient to develop and enhance those skills that are not affected fundamentally by the underlying problem (Mechanic 1977b).

In long-term care there are few basic principles that can be generalized across problem areas. One very important research finding, however, that has been reported consistently across disability areas is that inactivity, lack of participation, and dependence have an erosive effect on levels of social functioning, hopefulness, and a sense of human dignity (Wing 1962). There is nothing more destructive to the elderly, the mental patient, the retarded, or the physically handicapped than to remain inactive, uninvolved, and totally dependent on program personnel. It contributes to diminished levels of coping, loss of affect, and the development of an apathy syndrome. These observations have been buttressed by research on learned helplessness that suggests that persons who lose a sense of control over their environment develop a depressive-like syndrome and suffer physical deterioration and even death (Seligman 1975). Thus, the first requirement of any good program of long-term care is to make use of the potential of the disabled to meet their own needs, to assume as much responsibility over their own affairs as they can, and to participate in meaningful social encounters. The traditional medical-care system, however, reinforces dependence, passivity, and reliance on medical authority.

One of the ironies of national attempts to improve long-term care is the failure to work within sound rehabilitative principles and the pursuit of policies that reinforce a tendency toward the types of erosion of human capacity described above. The extension of benefits to the old and the disabled under such programs as Medicare and Medicaid has reinforced a hospital-based medical approach to the inevitable physical deterioration of old age and a focus on institutional care. Medicare provides considerable subsidy for dependent care in nursing homes, but only the most limited community care services for the frail elderly who wish to retain some independence and who require community assistance in doing so. Similarly, Medicaid has an institutional bias and, for example, provides funds for transfer of psychiatric patients to nursing homes, where they may receive largely custodial care, which reinforces the apathy syndrome (Stotsky 1970). Many of these patients are relatively young and potentially vigorous but are kept as quiet as possible to minimize supervision needs in the institution. Thus they may be put on heavy doses of drugs, induced to sit for hours on end in front of television sets, and discouraged from activities that demand supervision or that might present control problems. Similar funds invested in community care programs would have much greater social potential, but current funding mechanisms make such programs almost impossible to develop on any long-term basis.

There are forces, however, that will create pressures for change in the future, including the economic pressures resulting from the increasing proportion of elderly in the population. As noted above, the elderly will become a more important political pressure group, and as they gain political experience and sophistication, they will lobby effectively for a wider range of benefits. Also, with the emphasis on deinstitutionalization and on the ideology that all persons regardless of handicap should be assisted in achieving their social potential, there will be more demand for the development of community settings that facilitate such goals without disruptions to the community as a whole. Moreover, the courts are increasingly finding that custodial care without treatment is unacceptable and that communities have an obligation to provide persons with the least restrictive alternative necessary. Over the long range, these pressures will converge to create a climate in which experiments and innovations in financing of care become not only more feasible but also the appropriate political response.

The approach presently embodied in financing programs is no accident. First, extending financing to community programs involves a large number of new reimbursable providers, and no one as yet has a clear idea of what possible financial commitments might be necessary to achieve a reasonable pattern of care. Moreover, new services almost always attract new eligible clients, adding to the burden of financing services. Second, the alternatives themselves are only poorly developed and, with the exception of an occasional demonstration project, we have still to launch a major developmental effort. Faced with uncertainties, it is easier to follow the path of least resistance in continuing to finance the types of care structures that the community is familiar with and that have a certain legitimacy within the larger medical-care system. Third, although there are successful demonstrations of community care (Stein and Test 1978), we are uncertain of the ways to make comparable seeds flourish in other settings where it is difficult to replicate the same leadership, enthusiasm, and know-how. Unlike such technologies as the artificial kidney, which diffused very quickly once financing became available, the social technologies associated with long-term care are much more difficult to develop and require considerable coordinative ability. The organizational know-how required to set up a freestanding dialysis unit is both relatively simple and more consistent with dominant organizational patterns in the medical sector. There is more to solving the financial problems and organizational dilemmas than defining what we would like to do, and thus the remainder of this chapter focuses on these problems.

Stability in Funding

Any adequate organizational innovation requires not only start-up funding but also considerable stability of funding over some period of time. Although stability in funding is problematic for every organization, it is particularly acute for new organizational settings that depart from conventional professional roles, career lines, and legitimized patterns of performance. Thus, insecurities are likely to be greater, and when threats of instability exist there is more danger of losing talented personnel who become concerned about the viability of the organization. Although traditional organizations usually have financing alternatives through either the private marketplace or a variety of existing public programs, and some political clout to ensure continuing financing, new organizations are more at the mercy of their environments and therefore are much more fragile. Not having developed legitimacy and power that comes from building a political constituency, they have little countercontrol over a capricious environment that may cut the flow of funds at any time (Downs 1967). Moreover, during periods of financial stringency and budget cuts, it is these programs that have no supporting political base that are most easily reduced without political threat. Thus, without financial nurturance, new organizational settings have a high mortality rate.

Financial programs such as Medicare and Medicaid—and certainly national health insurance in future years—have the capability to build new organizational settings by the types of reimbursement structures they develop. Medicare and Medicaid, for example, resulted in an enormous enlargement of the nursing-home industry because they provided benefit dollars to provide for posthospital and long-term care. As financing became available, entrepreneurs and corporations moved into the nursing-home field, which had been almost exclusively dominated by small operators. In a relatively short time, there was an enormous increase in the capacity of the industry to accommodate patients, but not necessarily at an appropriate or reasonable level of care. Although a great deal must be done to improve care in nursing homes, which varies a great deal in quality, the fact is that this sector grew enormously in a short period of time when stable funding was promised. Nursing homes, however, were institutions developed along traditional lines that were easy to replicate. The problem of building community alternatives is more difficult.

A stable financial structure for community alternatives requires decisions on who should be reimbursed, under what conditions, and for what types of services. Although it is relatively easy to determine what one must pay for a day of nursing-home care, it is much more difficult to determine how to pay for a total pattern of services including medical care, day care, homemaker care, social support, social services, and recreational and activity programs. Indeed, the prospect seems frightening to program planners when they consider the wide range of possible services and program personnel that might be included as part of such a community approach.

One possible alternative to the open-ended nature of the problem is to develop contracts with community organizations to provide and coordinate the total pattern of care for elderly patients on a capitation basis. If the population contracted for was sufficiently large, it would be possible to make reasonable actuarial predictions as to costs and revenues and to plan a total integrated pattern of services that substitutes less-expensive services for more-expensive hospital and nursing-care services. Organizations that have the capitation contracts and who share some of the financial risks would have incentives for substituting less expensive community services for more expensive institutional services, for using a wider mix of personnel, substituting other types of manpower for the heavy utilization of physician services in this age group, and for maintaining the functional capacity of these patients instead of making them more dependent. To the extent that the handicapped continue to retain responsibility for their own functioning, they put less of a burden on the organization.

Old people who have many serious chronic problems will continue to require many medical services, but under existing financial incentives we tend to replace needed social services with medical care because this is what the programs pay for. By shifting the incentives it is possible to develop a more balanced program of medical and social care. Because the standards are uncertain, and there is a danger of underservice in capitation programs, considerable developmental effort will be necessary to develop criteria and measure standards of care in varying organizational settings. Designing new organizational settings is difficult, and thus funding in the beginning must include developmental costs that assist in building the necessary infrastructure. The challenge is difficult and the prospects uncertain, but we had better begin our efforts if we are to deal constructively with impending problems.

Considerable attention must be devoted also to the nursing-home sector. In developing this sector we have given much more attention to providing the beds needed to meet the demand generated by federal financing than to ensure that the services provided were of decent quality. Although it would have been relatively easy to establish stringent standards—and a great many standards were set— enforcing them created a serious dilemma characteristic of much regulation (Friedman 1968). To the extent that there was a shortage of beds, eliminating existing beds because they failed to meet certain criteria created more problems than it solved. Although such regulation may work successfully in an overdeveloped industry, it was counterproductive when the federal government was attempting to encourage operators to increase their bed capacity to accommodate new demand.

The nursing-home sector is now well established, and careful thought is necessary to develop incentives to improve the quality of care provided. Traditionally, nursing homes have been evaluated by their capacity to deliver varying levels of service as measured by the types of personnel employed. Measuring such inputs, however, never really assures that a high quality of care is actually provided. It would be more desirable to develop good programmatic standards and to link rates of reimbursement to them. Although emphasis in the past has been given to potential nursing and medical care, it might be more useful to consider standards consistent with maintaining the quality of social functioning and increasing independence among patients. Institutions that have developed programs to encourage patient involvement, activity, and responsibility would thus be reimbursed at higher rates than those that simply provide the more traditional services. How to ensure that the activities and programs developed are meaningful ones is an important task.

Nursing-home care suffers for a variety of reasons. Often the needs of old and sick patients are many, while the available financing is limited. Many of the big businesses and small entrepreneurs that dominate the industry are profit-oriented but lack a strong professional commitment to the problems of the aged. The pattern of necessary professional services is expensive because each of the relevant professionals demands high renumeration, resulting in a tendency either to cut down on the number of professional services or to provide only very perfunctory ones. In the last analysis, however, the quality of nursing-home care depends on the commitment of the staff who work there and the empathy and involvement they show; but most nursing-home jobs are seen as "dead-end" employment, drawing largely poor, uneducated, minority members, who are themselves often exploited, embittered, and cynical. Even under the best of circumstances, taking care of sick old people is difficult; when the workers are themselves alienated and frustrated, they often behave in a harsh and inhumane way, expressing against their dependent charges the bitterness that arises from economic and racial tensions in the larger society. In short, there is no quick and easy solution for developing humane nursing-home climates.

It has been suggested that one way of improving the quality of nursing homes is to link them with clinics, hospitals, and other medical institutions. Making such facilities responsible for the operation and supervision of nursing homes introduces a level of professional commitment and responsibility to the sick that is now sadly lacking. Although in principle such links and added supervision would be desirable, they would in all probability require a very large economic investment. Introducing the kind of standards good hospitals would deem necessary would be costly, and the medical bias of the medical institutions might reinforce an approach that is entirely too expensive for what it achieves. All of our experience to date suggests that any service organized and administered by physicians and hospitals will be priced very high, and if we should choose to go in this direction, it is unclear where the funds are to come from.

A more viable alternative from an economic point of view is to develop organizations that link care in nursing homes with community supportive care as part of one total system (Smits and Draper 1974). As health-maintenance organizations or regionalized health-care plans paid on a capitation basis develop, it becomes more possible to bring medical care, nursing-home care, and community supportive care under one organizational program that establishes an easier flow back and forth among various facilities as needs dictate. The British National Health Service, for example, facilitates keeping old people and handicapped persons in their families or homes by providing homemaker services, meals on wheels, day care, and activity programs. Hospital short-term beds are maintained to allow families caring for old persons to go on a short vacation or a weekend trip to give them some relief from the continuing responsibility. The knowledge that the system is there to help and will offer relief when needed increases the willingness of many families to assume the difficult responsibility of taking care of their aged.

To the extent that we can develop organizations to provide the entire range of services on the basis of an agreed-upon capitation, it would be possible, at least initially, on a demonstration basis, to forgo some of the usual federal program requirements that make it difficult to move patients back and forth in the total spectrum of care. Institutions, however, taking on responsibility for the total spectrum of care would have to develop the community-organization and social-welfare capacities necessary in addition to the more typical medical-care approaches. Many of the necessary approaches exist in Scandinavia and Europe, and we can learn a great deal from experience elsewhere. Although our different culture and form of social organization limit the utility of some of these models, they do include many components that could fit the American situation (Glasscote, Gudeman, and Miles 1977).

Whatever organizational alternatives we develop in the future, the problems of inhumane care will remain without concerted efforts to change the meanings associated with employment in nursing homes. This can be achieved to some extent by professionalizing such work, but not without considerable additional cost. Another alternative would be to put greater emphasis on marshaling volunteer services to supplement existing services and sustaining them through programs of training, recognition, and rewards for excellent service among both volunteers and nursing-home staff. Volunteer services are difficult to maintain, however, and such volunteers often lack the commitment to continuing responsibility, reliability, and persistence that is necessary in the care of the sick aged person. If organized effectively, however, and if given sufficient visibility and status, such volunteer programs have a great deal to contribute. If nothing else, the presence of volunteers will contain the harshest and most inhumane aspects of care, and, from a political standpoint, if enough people see firsthand the conditions of care for our old, sick citizens, then political pressures for improved care will mount.

The Fragility of Organizational Alternatives

It is extremely difficult to sustain the vitality of new organizational settings, and thus their fragile nature requires considerable nurturance (Sarason 1972). All the pressures of financing, professionalization, and the desire to minimize environmental uncertainty push innovations back toward the mainstream of care or limit their longevity. The factors that facilitate the development of new alternatives are quite different from those that allow them to prosper and take root in different settings, and thus the problem is not simply one of development but also of successful diffusion once it is demonstrated that a program really works.

As a starting point, new alternatives originate with mavericks, persons who are dissatisfied with current types of practice and who are willing to take risks in trying something new. To launch the type of community program under discussion, one needs a fairly ambitious and aggressive administrator who can command the initial financial resources, who can attract other talented persons to share the risks involved in a new venture, and who can negotiate the community agreements needed. The negotiating ability is essential to carry out programmatic tasks, to sell the program to groups in the community that might be threatened by the program and thus sabotage it, and to create a favorable political climate generally. Although the relative importance of these skills will depend on the nature of the program, its intraorganizational requirements, and its public visibility, some efforts along these lines are always necessary for any program that functions outside the walls of an institution. Any effective community care program for mental patients, for example, must work out arrangements with the neighborhood in which it functions, the facilities it depends on, and the political officials and the police, who are in a continuing position either to assist or to destroy the program (Mechanic 1973).

Development of new community settings also typically involves using professionals and other personnel in new roles, bypassing conventional routines. This is often unsettling, and such personnel need considerable support and reassurance. They also must feel that the extra efforts required are worth it, and thus a charismatic administrator is desirable in the beginning to build the necessary commitment and momentum. Although such an administrator may build sufficient enthusiasm and involvement to recruit excellent personnel, these personnel must often forgo the security that follows more conventional types of work and more recognized career patterns. Innovations provide a certain excitement and sense of being on the cutting edge, but they also involve risks. Unlike those in more conventional and established organizations, career lines for persons in new settings become less clear, and should the innovation fail they may be limited in future career options. Thus, while the initial enthusiasm of a new idea may attract talented people, there are inevitable frustrations and losses from the organization, and it takes considerable ingenuity to maintain the original momentum. In addition, long-term-care patients are often difficult to work with, suffer from problems that are relatively intractable, and are frequently defined as patients of low prestige. As the initial excitement of a new approach wanes, personnel develop routines and patterned responses that are more consistent with their own needs for certainty and predictable rewards, and the innovative program becomes more like conventional practice.

If public policies are to establish truly innovative means of dealing with the sociomedical needs of patients, they will have to provide the nurturance for long-term growth. It is simply not enough to provide short-term seed monies on the assumption that these programs will support themselves after a short period of development. There must be clear prospect for continued stable funding, because the clients or advocates of such organizations are unlikely to be able to support their continuance. Moreover, without some assurance of continued support, these organizations are likely to lose their most talented personnel and much of the momentum that contributes to effectiveness.

High-Priority Research Areas

We obviously know too little about how to develop new organizational settings in a way that allows them to flourish and multiply. While some new settings become successfully established, at least for a time, they are difficult to replicate (Fairweather 1978). Those who initiate innovations have a greater stake in their success than those who simply copy them, and the development and maintenance of momentum in any new program over any extended period of time are formidable problems. We need a better understanding of the conditions under which new settings are most likely to flourish and the techniques through which successful innovations can be replicated. Although we know a great deal about the diffusion of specific agricultural, technical, and social practices (Rogers 1962), the transferability of complex organizational arrangements is more difficult. Social organizational innovations dependent on a complex intraorganizational environment rely on complex negotiations and coordination, which may be different in every area depending on the existing political and social structure.

At the patient-care level we still have a great deal to learn about the best way to fit different patterns of service to the specific disabilities patients have. Although we have learned some techniques that effectively limit disability and favorably affect the course of long-term illness, we still lack a great deal of fundamental knowledge necessary to develop the specificity of services required for a truly successful approach.

Further, we require techniques that allow institutionalization of new approaches without so bureaucratizing services and so cementing roles that flexibility becomes impossible. Most new organizations seem to have a limited period of vitality before taking on certain conservative and bureaucratic characteristics, and increasingly union contracts make it very difficult, even initially, to ensure flexibility. We know too little about the way to maintain a sense of liveliness and excitement over time in any social program. One technique is obviously through recruitment and retention policies that bring young energetic persons with new ideas into the organization. But agencies for long-term care also require considerable continuity of service and personnel, and the proper balance and needed trade-offs are unclear.

Whatever the uncertainties, one thing is fully clear: long-term care will become an increasingly important area and one fraught with financial and organizational problems. The prudent course is to invest now in serious problem definition and conceptualization, research and demonstration, and program evaluation. Although many uncertainties will undoubtedly remain, we must achieve a better definition of our options and the ways to promote them. The quality of our lives in the future will depend on it.

6 | Community Integration of the Mentally Ill

The chronic mental patient constitutes the largest category of seriously handicapped persons requiring long-term community planning. In the past two decades there has been a dramatic shift in the auspices of care for the mentally ill. Economic pressures on state institutions, social ideologies, social-science research, and civil liberties advocacy have all converged to discourage unnecessary hospitalization and to reduce significantly the resident populations of public mental hospitals. Resident populations in state and county mental hospitals peaked at almost 559,000 in 1955, declining gradually to 191,000 in 1975 (U.S. President's Commission on Mental Health 1978). While the development of psychoactive drugs in the middle 1950s assisted this trend in changing attitudes of professionals and families about the control of psychopathology and helped alleviate some of the more bizarre and frightening symptoms of psychosis, the changes attest to the powerful impact of social ideology and administrative outlook in the provision of medical care.

The introduction of psychoactive drugs was obviously helpful, but there is considerable evidence that it was neither a necessary nor a sufficient condition to explain the major social changes that occurred. In some localities the shift to community care had already begun prior to the introduction of new drugs, and in others large numbers of patients were released from hospitals to communities without continuing drug therapy (Mechanic 1969). Moreover, the trend in deinstitutionalization involved not only the mentally ill but also the retarded, juvenile offenders, and other social deviants (Scull 1977). If any single factor was crucial in allowing large numbers of dependent persons to return to community living and to institutions

64

other than mental hospitals, it was the development of financial programs that subsidized increased welfare assistance, medical care, and payment to nursing homes. With Medicare and Medicaid there was a major shift in resident patients from mental hospitals to nursing homes so that by the late 1960s such patients in nursing homes exceeded those in mental institutions, and this shift was evident for those below sixty-five years of age as well as for older patients (U.S. President's Commission on Mental Health 1978). The change is somewhat deceptive, however, because some institutions changed their status from mental hospitals to nursing homes as reimbursement policies shifted. This statistical artifact is indicative of other patterns in deinstitutionalization that have been obfuscated by the optimistic rhetoric that has characterized much of the commentary on the care of the mentally ill.

In the past two decades patterns of psychiatric care have altered appreciably. In 1955, 49 percent of all psychiatric episodes involved state and county mental hospitals, but this declined to 9 percent in 1975. Outpatient psychiatric services and those provided by mental-health centers accounted for 76 percent of all episodes in 1975 as compared with 23 percent in 1955 (U.S. President's Commission on Mental Health 1978). While the number of patients admitted to mental hospitals actually increased until the early 1970s, length of stay fell sufficiently to contribute to reduced resident populations. The growing availability of care on an outpatient basis and increased subsidy and insurance coverage to pay for it in large part explain the rise of episodes of care from 1.7 million in 1955 to 6.4 million in 1975.

Concepts of Deinstitutionalization

Despite these very positive changes in the availability and auspices of care, profound problems remain, particularly in respect to the most chronically disabled patients. The concept of deinstitutionalization masks as much as it reveals, and often it reflects little more than reduction of resident populations and associated costs. Frequently deinstitutionalization has offered limited alternatives for the ill and dependent who face difficult problems of community adaptation. Ideally, however, deinstitutionalization should be viewed as an integrated set of social policies designed to promote a reasonable level of functioning among the handicapped with the fewest possible restrictions on their mobility and social participation. If carried out effectively, deinstitutionalization offers possibilities for significantly improving the quality of life of handicapped persons while conserving social resources, but if executed seriously it offers no simple panacea for the escalating costs of medical, psychiatric, and socially related care for impaired and chronic patients.

The term deinstitutionalization as it is most commonly used describes the movement of patient populations from large public institutions to other locations and the substitution of community treatment or short-term institutional care for long-term custody. However, the term has also been used to refer to the transfer of patients from one institution to another, such as the movement of patients from mental hospitals to nursing homes, board and care facilities, and other sheltered living situations. The concept thus is vague and ambiguous and confuses institutional transfer with independent community living. It also fails to distinguish the impact of different settings on the quality of living and social functioning experienced by patients with varying problems and disabilities (U.S. National Institute of Mental Health 1976).

The erosive effects of dependent custodial life on the skills and capacities of patients have been known for a very long time (Scull 1977). Moreover, the role of institutional environments in inducing violent inclinations and other secondary reactions not inherent in the primary problems from which patients suffered has also been observed by both clinicians and researchers (Eaton and Weil 1955). In the 1950s and 1960s various studies documented that long tenure in institutions and dependence on institutional services were associated with a syndrome of apathy, hopelessness, and incapacity (Wing 1962). The syndrome was called "institutionalism" and was seen as having three interrelated components (Wing 1967). First, long-term patients were not only ill, but often lacked strong ties with community, family, or work, and were vulnerable in addition because of age, poverty, and lack of social interests and ties. Second, there are those elements of disability that result more directly from the disease process itself and may become exacerbated with time unless rehabilitative efforts are made to reverse the process. Third are the erosive effects of the institution itself, such as the consequences that flow from lack of activity, participation, independence, and a sense of involvement.

The institutionalism syndrome, thus, was not a characteristic of any particular institution but a culmination of a variety of social conditions that could vary a great deal from one institution to another, or even from one community context to another, including families, neighborhoods, and community care facilities. While the traditional mental hospital or training institution for the retarded provided poor and inadequate care for the most part, as conditions improved the better institutions provided more professional service, organized therapeutic activities, and patient involvement than are ordinarily found in many nursing homes or board and care facilities. These residences often provide little professional care or even supervision, and patients may remain socially isolated and inactive (Segal and Aviram 1978; Stotsky 1970). They often become highly dependent on the operator of the facility, exercising even less control over their own lives than was common in the mental hospital. Still other patients return to rooms and apartments having no employment, few friends or social ties, and few community support structures that assist coping efforts or help prevent further deterioration.

Although a great deal of exhortation has been devoted to the idea that patients would return to their families and reestablish prior social ties, many patients are incapable of doing so, and families are often unreceptive. Thus, many patients released from mental hospitals formed "colonies" in the immediate area of the hospital, often arousing community hostility and an unfavorable political and social climate. The community resettlement of patients already highly institutionalized as a result of long tenure in hospitals, or others on irregular or no medication, resulted in an increased incidence of bizarre behaviors in public places which were frightening, embarrassing, or annoying to the community. Some communities became increasingly inhospitable, and a few even passed ordinances with the intent of keeping mental patients out of the area, although the courts have opposed such actions.

The problems described above need not occur, but they have been unfortunately common. These instances that have received a great deal of attention in the mass media, however, should not cloud the fact that many patients lead satisfactory and much improved lives in the community. We require a much clearer understanding of the types of community settings, residential living situations, and medical and social services that are appropriate for varying types of chronic and handicapped patients. Most discussions of deinstitutionalization are misleading in their failure to differentiate the impact of varying community settings on the quality of life of patients and the course of their illnesses and handicaps.

Both institutions and community settings provide a range of possible options that vary in cost depending on programmatic aspects. Although the release of patients to the community is always less expensive in direct costs than other alternatives if this is all that is done, other costs may be large: required welfare expenditures and indirect social costs to the patients, their families, and the community, measured by patient deterioration, disruption of family life, and problems of social control. Effective community care requires not only adequate medical services and the provision of supportive services, but also efforts in teaching patients coping skills that enhance their social capacities and life satisfactions.

In a carefully controlled study executed by Stein, Test, and their colleagues (1976), a thorough cost-benefit analysis was undertaken comparing patients randomly assigned to an excellent progressive inpatient hospital unit with those assigned to a training program in community living that emphasized the acquisition of coping skills and social supports. From a psychiatric and social standpoint the community patients performed better and reported greater life satisfactions than those treated in the hospital unit, although even the hospital patients spent most of the follow-up period in community settings. What primarily differentiated the two settings was the aggressive program in community living associated with the experimental venture that taught patients simple living skills and responsibility for their actions. On the economic side, when both direct and indirect financial costs are taken into account, the total care provided by the experiment in community living cost somewhat more than the in-hospital care ($8,093 to $7,296) (Weisbrod, Test, and Stein 1977), despite the fact that in the experimental group there was almost no use of hospitals.

The above is not a study of deinstitutionalization but more correctly an assessment of deinstitutionalization alternatives. In each case the issue is not long-term hospitalization but rather the value of dealing with acute episodes with short-term hospitalization or an ongoing community program. While the more conventional group received excellent hospital treatment during acute episodes, the experimental group had a more continuous community program. From a policy standpoint, however, the issue is the total impact of programs on people's lives and the ways to finance more effective programs. However effective programs like the above are demonstrated to be, they have little chance to develop and replicate unless an adequate and stable source of funding can be established.

In many discussions of cost affecting deinstitutionalization, there tends to be confusion between total costs and the way such costs are budgeted. Because the handicapped are supported by a variety of categorical programs developed by federal, state, and local governments, calculations of costs are frequently made in terms of a particular budget such as the funds available for the mental-health program of a state or locality. For example, a patient in a state mental hospital is a cost charged to the state mental-health budget; if the patient is transferred to a nursing home, the costs of care may be charged against the state Medicaid program, involving a large transfer of cost to the federal government, because Medicaid is a federal-state matching program. Similarly, a patient returned to the community who has no job and requires welfare, food stamps, and other governmental payments may no longer be a charge to the mental-health system but may require as much or more public support as before. While it may be advantageous to a particular program or agency to transfer costs to another unit of government or to another level of government, in the aggregate it may be no less costly to the public. Although the structure of financing for the handicapped makes a certain amount of "ping-ponging" of patients astute bureaucratic policy, it may not be in the best interests of the patients involved and may in addition confuse the public as to what it is paying to pursue alternative social policies in caring for the handicapped.

While the financing problems of community programs involving social and educational services as well as traditional medical services are widely known, there is considerable fear on the part of administrators of broadening services in a way that may attract new practitioners as well as new clients and further contribute to the escalation of the costs of care chargeable to governmental budgets or insurance policies (Mechanic 1978d). The funding made available beyond usual medical care, thus, is in the form of categorical grants to programs and agencies such as community mental-health centers, university psychiatry departments, and state and local mental-health agencies. When such funding is agency-oriented rather than client-oriented, it tends to segment further an already highly fragmented service sector in which interdependent programming is extraordinarily difficult to achieve. Some form of capitation financing is needed in which a large agency or a consortium of agencies accepts full responsibility for programming the entire spectrum of in-hospital and community services for the mentally ill with incentives for developing appropriate community educational and support structures.

Dilemmas in Community Care

Deinstitutionalization is not simply a matter of cost, or even a matter of what professionals and patients might wish. It is a social process influenced by ideologies, trends in civil liberties, conflicting conceptions of freedom and rehabilitation, and trade-offs between the choices of clients and what the state conceives to be in their interests. The courts, for example, are increasingly moving toward the doctrine of the "least restrictive alternative" in the involuntary care of the mentally ill and retarded populations, but with little adequate conceptualization of what this entails or how it can be accomplished. What might appear as less restrictive to judges, lawyers, and middle-class professionals who have had little contact with many treatment contexts might be quite different from what patients actually experience.

We have come to associate large institutions with impersonal, degrading, and restrictive practices, a reputation many have unfortunately earned. Such institutions when they are well run, however, provide opportunities to develop programs absent in many smaller settings (Allen 1974). Such institutions may also offer patients considerably more personal freedom than that offered in small board and care facilities and nursing homes in which operators completely control the lives of patients, interfere with their privacy and personal rights, and strictly control their activities. Moreover, the perception of a hospital environment depends on the patient's community living situation. Lawrence Linn (1968), for example, in a study of mental-hospital patients, found that many lower-class patients facing financial and social difficulties in the community perceived the mental hospital as a helpful respite, offering them more personal freedom than they had outside. For many older chronic patients with long tenure in mental hospitals, the outside world may offer frightening prospects compared with the types of adaptations they have achieved in the hospital context. Similarly, while nursing homes may appear as more benign and less restrictive settings than mental hospitals for patients unable to survive independently, such institutions are less likely to offer the special services, professional assistance, and independence that a well-run mental hospital can provide. The point is not that we should return to dependence on mental hospitals, good or bad, but that we must guard against confusing appearances with realities.

Deinstitutionalization has been accompanied by a strong social ethic of personal freedom and independent living, reflected in our social policies. Moreover, many patients share these concepts of personal autonomy even if the consequences for them may seem negative from an independent view. Although there has been great criticism of the alleged "dumping" of mental patients by large mental institutions and allegations of victimization and despair suffered by these patients, most seem to prefer community living despite the unfavorable conditions (Leaf 1978). While some obviously would welcome returning to a hospital and should have a safe refuge, those who value community tenure despite the many harsh realities require careful planning and assistance. The balance between the rights of patients to be left alone if they wish against the demands of communities to be protected from bizarre and disruptive behavior is difficult to achieve but becomes more possible with the development of programs combining necessary medical, educational, and social services (Stein and Test 1978).

At the level of the mental hospital we face a difficult dilemma. Communities in the vicinity of mental hospitals are often hostile to the colonization of mental patients in their areas. Moreover, the communities and the institutions resist the closure of the hospital or the transfer of funds to other programs because careers and jobs depend on it, and the communities are reluctant to give up the economic base that institutions provide. Traditional hospital employees thus constitute a strong reactionary force. With the effective unionization of hospital employees and the political influence this brings, it becomes enormously difficult to alter financial allocations fundamentally. Unless effective ways can be developed for retraining hospital workers and ensuring their employment in alternative efforts more consistent with new mental-health policies, such employees will continue to be a vigorous source of resistance to change and use their influence to thwart alternatives. If these workers can be retrained to provide supportive and educational services in the community to patients, this may not only serve the mentally ill better but align the interests of patients and staff in the same direction.

It is quite natural that patients settle in the immediate community of hospitals when they have no close social ties and some
dependence on future services. In one sense this is an advantage
because it facilitates the outreach of the hospital and the development of community programs, and many patients are dependent on
the social supports and services that such programs are likely to
offer. Moreover, visibly handicapped patients, such as many chronic
schizophrenics, are likely to be excluded from more advantageous
social settings, and even if they can successfully pass as normal they
are likely to be socially isolated and without obvious sponsors.
Administrators, aware of community resistance, tend to follow the
path of least resistance, locating facilities in areas offering the least
political opposition.

The location of facilities for the mentally ill, the handicapped,
and other stigmatized patients involves difficult choices. While central city areas may not be the most desirable living sites, they usually
offer access to transportation and other facilities that are needed by
the handicapped. They also offer a context in which there is greater
toleration and less stigmatization, reducing certain kinds of burdens
on the lives of these residents. To the extent that persons needing
special services are concentrated, it is easier to provide accessible
social services and other social supports. But while such environments may be pragmatically optimal, they offer a less attractive
physical environment, greater risks of crime and other types of
victimization, and perhaps an inability as well to escape from a
community of handicapped persons. Thus, such communities do not
reintegrate the handicapped into the "normal community," but that
may not be possible in any case.

In contrast, the dispersion of handicapped people in the community decreases visibility and reduces community impact and reaction, but also makes it more difficult to provide essential services
these persons may need. Dispersion makes it more possible to achieve
reintegration into the community without producing an alarm reaction. Perhaps the most important factor for community integration
of the handicapped is the acceptance of them by the community
(Segal and Aviram 1978), but such acceptance is reduced as they
constitute a larger group and have a more visible presence, particularly in suburban neighborhoods. The visible presence of handicapped people in ordinary social settings over time, however, probably contributes to a "normalization" of their presence if incidents

do not occur and if community groups concerned with the issue do not become polarized.

While many handicapped persons may require continued special services of one sort or another depending on their particular disabilities, they also require a reasonable degree of integration into a larger community, where they can be accepted on their own terms without suffering stigma, where they have reasonable opportunities to participate in community activities and use community resources, and where they receive some warmth and social support from the community. These conditions are often difficult to achieve in suburban communities without obvious sponsorship. There is a great potential here for voluntary efforts on the part of community organizations in extending to the handicapped opportunities to participate as fully as possible in community affairs as individuals and not as a category of disabled persons. Patients with the most personal resources and fewest visible handicaps often prefer to avoid other impaired persons and live a more ordinary life in the community. While this is desirable to the extent possible, such patients often become isolated from services and often fail to make contact when they require help. Being unobtrusive yet helpful and aggressive at the appropriate times is an extraordinarily difficult task in the light of such values as autonomy, privacy, and personal rights. It can be executed successfully only when there is a strong sense of trust and close personal ties between client and helper and when the client has a sense that the helper has something truly useful to give.

Deinstitutionalization and Community

While the concept of community is often associated with psychiatric care outside the hospital, little attention has been given to what the patient's community really was. To some it was simply a synonym for any location outside the hospital, for others a synonym for a return to prior family settings. For many patients, return to family settings was neither viable nor therapeutic, and patients were located in a wide variety of settings in communities but were not necessarily part of them.

Community is both a social and a psychological construct. It refers to patterned relationships among persons and to a sense of being part of the pattern—a sense of identity. Given the character of

American urban communities, even the ordinary citizen with job and family may psychologically feel a lack of belonging or integration. How much more difficult it must be, then, for an isolated mental patient without family or stable employment, handicapped by incapacities and economic difficulties, and often stigmatized as well. Lack of social belonging is a source of strain and loneliness, and integration may serve as an important buffer against the stresses associated with daily life. Social integration provides not only belonging and meaning but also a variety of tangible and symbolic supports that make life easier. While there is a consensus that social-support systems are essential, there is relatively little agreement as to the ways such support can be effectively provided. Certainly they include such tangible assets as the sharing of resources, assistance, and time. But they also involve communication that a person is valued, cared for, and esteemed.

It should be obvious that putting patients in the community is quite different than providing them with a sense of community, an outcome which is only rarely achieved with the chronically mentally ill. Experience suggests that these patients, like other deviants, develop their own subculture with defined locations where they eat, occasionally meet one another, and spend some of their time, which may weigh heavily upon them. In these settings patients are tolerated and accepted and may even find sponsors who offer friendship, assistance, and some relief from loneliness. The process of forming a community, however, is sporadic and uncertain and not very satisfying at the very best. Efforts must be made to assist patients to become part of ongoing communities or to form their own, and this constitutes an important aspect of community programs that seek to improve the quality of patients' lives. It can be achieved, however, only if financing for the mentally ill provides incentives for community programming as well as for individual service.

7 | Mental-Health Benefits under National Health Insurance

The design of mental-health benefits under national health insurance (NHI) poses a variety of policy issues that are not readily resolved by available empirical evidence. If the issue of what benefits should be covered is viewed largely as a technical problem, then the rich experience of the private and nonprofit insurance sector in extending mental-health benefits is instructive (Follman 1970). But if the policy questions are construed more broadly to cover such issues as the relationship of provision of care to need, the distributive effects of mental-health benefits, and the means to promote a more effective and efficient pattern of services, then the necessary analysis is far more complex. If our concern is not only with the insurance sector but with the implications of NHI for the total pattern of mental-health care, then we must take into account how such a program might affect financing of other programs at the federal, state, and local levels as well.

Difficulties arise at the start from the fact that our knowledge of the etiologies and treatments of most mental disorders remains uncertain, and the relative advantages of traditional patterns of psychiatric care as compared with alternative interventions are unclear. Moreover, disagreements continue about the appropriate boundaries for differentiating mental illnesses from the abundant frustrations, problems, and disillusionments that people suffer in the ordinary course of everyday life; and there are those who still persist in their claims that mental illness is simply a metaphor for deviant behavior (Szasz 1974) and that the mental-disease concept is a myth (Rosenhan 1973). In areas in which the experts have such diverse conceptions of the nature of disorder and appropriate treatment, it is not surprising that policymakers approach such concerns with some confusion.

Despite the conceptual difficulties, there has been in recent years considerable expansion of mental-health benefits under private and nonprofit insurance coverage (Reed, Myers, and Scheidemandel 1972). The typical approach, as in the general medical area, has been to define as legitimate illnesses whatever conditions are treated by the designated experts—most usually psychiatrists but occasionally psychologists and psychiatric social workers as well. Thus, the third parties avoid the quagmire of attempting to define insurable illness and leave this to clinical judgment. Instead, when benefits have been expanded, the insurers have protected themselves from unanticipated costs by imposing relatively high coinsurance and deductibles and limiting numbers of visits, allowable fees for each consultation, and total benefits covered. With growth of confidence based on extensive experience, hospital coverage for mental-health problems has improved substantially, although most insurers remain cautious relative to outpatient psychiatric care.

The present insurance structure for mental-health coverage that has evolved has been a pragmatic response to pressures for greater coverage from insured groups and has not been initiated with the intent either to develop the most rational pattern of psychiatric insurance or to improve the mental-health-care delivery system as a whole. The response of the private sector has been largely incremental, working around the existing pattern of care. NHI, in contrast, involves policies affecting the entire nation, and the impact of the benefit structure on the delivery system is a crucial consideration. The pattern of mental-health benefits under NHI will largely establish the future form of mental-health services in the community, the types of personnel available, and the relationships between the general medical and mental-health sectors.

The extension of psychiatric benefits under insurance had important implications for the distribution of care. It followed and may have reinforced an existing trend toward providing services to groups in the population who needed them the least. The most comprehensive insurance coverage is frequently available to the most advantaged segments of the working population, and even among those with comparable insurance coverage, persons with higher incomes, education, and greater sophistication use the most services (Avnet 1962), despite the inverse relationship between socioeconomic status and mental-health impairment (Dohrenwend and Dohrenwend 1969;

1974). One study found, for example, that insured persons with college degrees as compared with those with an education of grade school or less were six times as likely to seek psychiatric care, and they used office psychotherapy visits almost ten times as often as those less educated (Avnet 1962:90, 97). Experience with educated groups receptive to psychotherapy suggests that when there are few deductibles and coinsurance provisions, they will use a large number of psychotherapy services. Moreover, these patients who have greater financial resources are better able to absorb whatever cost-sharing features are involved in obtaining such care and thus are less inhibited from using available benefits.

Use of insurance coverage, of course, also depends on the geographic and social accessibility of care. Psychiatrists and psychotherapists are disproportionately located in urban centers and affluent areas and are socially more receptive to educated and verbal clients, resulting in different degrees of access among persons having comparable insurance benefits. Differentials in the availability of psychiatrists between metropolitan, rural, and central city areas may be twenty- to thirtyfold (Brown 1977:13). Providers more available to the poor, including social workers, counselors, and other nonmedical personnel, have been typically excluded from third-party reimbursement. What needs are insured for, as noted earlier, depends on the professional consulted, and this results in an inconsistency in the receipt of benefits among persons with comparable problems and insurance. The affluent and sophisticated are more likely to understand the system and to make sure that they receive services from professionals eligible for reimbursement. Limitations on the definition of appropriate personnel to provide mental-health care may allow the sophisticated patient to receive reimbursement for many minor problems while treatment by nonmedical personnel directed to more serious conditions may not be paid for.

It is not difficult, however, to understand the reluctance of insurers to expand the definition of reimbursable providers of mental-health care in any open-ended way, because such personnel significantly outnumber the approximately 28,000 psychiatrists. If there is anything we know well in the health-services field, it is that the availability of supply in the absence of fee barriers dramatically affects demand.

In 1972 the American Psychological Association sent questionnaires to some 62,000 individuals eligible for membership in their organization, of whom 35,361 responded. More than 10,000 listed clinical psychology as their specialty, and an additional 3,528 listed counseling psychology (U.S. Health Resources Administration 1975:255). Using the doctoral record files, the National Academy of Sciences estimated that there were 8,377 clinical psychologists at the doctoral level in 1973 (Commission on Human Resources 1976:41). In 1974 there were approximately 195,000 social workers in the United States, with more than 24,000 working in psychiatric settings (U.S. Health Resources Administration 1975:277). There were 7,210 full-time-equivalent social work staff in outpatient psychiatric clinics, and the potentialities for expansion of this group are very large under favorable reimbursement conditions. Moreover, there were more than 12,000 occupational therapists in the United States in 1974, of whom 8,000 were active (U.S. Health Resources Administration 1975:212). There are also numerous nurses with psychiatric skills who could effectively provide certain types of specialized care. It has been estimated that there are 121,000 psychiatrists, psychologists, psychiatric social workers, and psychiatric nurses in the United States at the present time (Brown 1977:3).

There are potentialities for using these personnel more efficiently in a variety of mental-health settings if satisfactory means of reimbursement for their services can be established. Although it would be foolhardy to extend the availability of reimbursement too broadly, a system of paying for psychiatric services on a capitation basis will encourage health organizations to seek a more efficient mix of therapeutic and rehabilitative personnel. Developing the necessary organizational arrangements to accomplish this will take time, but the structure of benefits developed under NHI should be consistent with this possibility.

The present insurance structure, which includes broader coverage for inpatient care for mental illness, provides incentives for "unnecessary" hospital care and encourages a medical approach to mental-health problems in contrast to community alternatives and educational and rehabilitative models. Such incentives turn attention away from the long-term requirements of the most impaired psychiatric patients who are in need of continuing community care services and whose needs are not covered by existing insurance programs. Insurance that reinforces traditional and expensive forms of individual treatment within a medical psychotherapeutic orientation provides little encouragement for the development of innovative community options using new types of organizational arrangements and personnel. Moreover, the mirage that insurance adequately provides coverage for mental-health needs may erode the political support necessary to encourage the development of patterns of community mental-health care for patients with chronic mental illness and high levels of impairment.

In short, we have developed insurance programs for psychiatric benefits that effectively limit total expenditures for psychiatric services, but also reinforce traditional, ineffective, and inefficient patterns of mental-health care, inhibit innovation and use of less-expensive mental-health personnel, and reinforce a medical rather than a social or educational approach to patients' psychological problems. The risk we face with the new opportunity for extending psychiatric benefits under NHI is that a poorly designed scheme may help to fix in place some of the weakest features of our existing mental-health delivery system.

In contrast, increased insurance coverage for mental-health problems can be a major advance if we keep in mind that such benefits are only one element of a coherent mental-health policy. Most existing services for impaired patients are provided by a variety of categorical programs supported by federal, state, and local authorities, including mental hospitals and community mental-health centers. Moreover, because most of the chronically disabled are poor, many of their needs are financed through welfare and other social agencies. Adequate cash assistance, for example, is a crucial component of any deinstitutionalization program (Scull 1977). Medicare and Medicaid not only provide medical and psychiatric care for eligible recipients but also facilitate the transfer of many chronic mental patients to other health-care settings. This should alert us to concern ourselves with financing in general and also with the implications of alternative financial arrangements for rehabilitation. A narrow or technical view of the insurance issue will not serve the mentally ill well.

An Epidemiological Approach to Psychiatric Need

Examining the way patients with a range of problems flow from the community into different service contexts is useful in assessing the dimensions of need for care (Lewis, Fein, and Mechanic 1976). Simply assessing service utilization of particular types of facilities such as psychiatric hospitalization or outpatient psychotherapy fails to map the variety of problems people face or their different means of coping with them. Although the epidemiological picture is incomplete because of the difficulty of adequately defining mental illness in community settings and because few studies examine more than one or two alternative treatment resources, the limited data available are instructive.

Community epidemiologic studies vary a great deal in case definition, but most find a large reservoir of problems characterized by depression, anxiety, psychophysiologic discomforts, insomnia, unhappiness, and alienation (U.S. President's Commission on Mental Health 1978). Although most of these problems do not constitute psychiatric disorders as conventionally defined, many of these persons suffer significantly and feel a need for assistance. At any point in time such persons may constitute as much as one-quarter of the population, but this estimate includes both mild and more serious disturbance. Unfortunately, we have too little understanding of the natural history of these symptoms and the benefits to be gained from varying levels of support and treatment. We do know, however, that there is considerable overlap in symptoms between those treated in a variety of outpatient settings and those who receive no treatment at all.

Although the appropriate treatment of such persons is not established, large numbers of them are found in primary medical-care settings (Shepherd, Cooper, Brown, and Kalton 1966). Physicians feel at a loss in knowing how to deal appropriately with these patients, and only a small minority are ever referred for specialized care. Those who come or are referred to psychiatric settings tend to have more severe symptoms and social and cultural orientations that enhance their receptivity to psychiatric care (Greenley and Mechanic 1976). The majority of patients, however, receive whatever treatment they obtain from primary-care physicians. Estimates vary a great deal as to what proportion of patients in general medical settings suffer from these types of symptoms, but there is wide agreement that they constitute a considerable burden of demand on ambulatory-care facilities (Andersen, Francis, Lion, and Daughety 1977). The distress associated with these patients' problems triggers a demand for medical service (Tessler, Mechanic, and Dimond 1976), and such patients are often recipients of intensive medical and surgical care that achieves little of value. Support, reassurance, and relief of suffering through pharmacological intervention, in contrast, are of some use. Although psychoactive drugs are used extensively in medical practice (Parry, Balter, Mellinger, Cisin, and Manheimer 1973), we do not know very much about when they are used. The mild tranquilizers such as Valium and Librium are among the most frequently used drugs in ordinary medical practice, and many of the prescriptions of barbiturates, amphetamines, and other commonly used drugs are a response to the distress syndromes described.

While experts debate whether the psychoactive drugs are used too readily or too sparingly (Gardner 1974), the implications of drug use without adequate monitoring for patients with high levels of distress are not trivial. Murphy (1975a; 1975b) found, for example, that 71 to 91 percent of patients who committed suicide had been under the recent care of a physician. Over two-thirds of these patients had histories of suicide threats or attempts, but these suicide gestures were known to only two-fifths of the physicians who provided care for them. There was evidence that three-quarters of the patients were depressed, but this diagnosis was rarely made by nonpsychiatrists nor was the depression treated. More than one-half of those who died by overdose had an unlimited prescription of the substance ingested or had received a prescription within a week or less before their deaths.

Whatever mental-health benefits are provided under NHI, it is inevitable that most services for common mental-health problems will be provided within the general medical sector by nonpsychiatrists. These problems are common and are often associated with physical symptoms and discomforts, and the patients involved may resist a psychological definition of their distress (Mechanic 1972c). Such patients frequently refuse referral to mental-health agencies or practitioners and tend to shop among physicians when they feel the medical care received is unresponsive. Any effective system of primary-medical-care services must take account of such patients in some fashion. However physicians may wish to limit their responsibilities and the scope of their work, such patients will continue to constitute a significant component of patient demand.

From a public-policy perspective, it would be neither productive nor economical to attempt to shift these patients to more specialized care. We have no evidence of the effectiveness of such care in most instances, and such a shift would take away scarce resources from patients with more profound psychological disabilities who need the available specialized services. Planning to ensure that patients with distress syndromes receive supportive assistance from the general medical sector is highly desirable, however. This can be facilitated by improving the capacity of primary-care practitioners to recognize more reliably such common problems as depression, alcoholism, and anxiety and by increasing their confidence in their ability to deal with such patients. Perhaps most important, primary-care physicians must improve their pharmacological knowledge of psychoactive drugs. More effort than at present can also be given to developing a consultant-psychiatrist role for primary care to provide backup assistance to practitioners in dealing with mental-health problems (Patrick, Eagle, and Coleman 1978). Also, as physicians become organized to a larger extent in groups and prepaid practices, it will become easier to integrate nonphysician mental-health personnel into primary care to provide counseling, supportive care, and behavior therapy and to assist in organizing and coordinating self-help and group-help efforts. Federal efforts can be of assistance by providing incentives for these developments and by funding demonstration programs and evaluations to ascertain the feasibility of varying approaches and to work out implementation problems.

Although efforts must be made to integrate more of psychiatric care within the mainstream of medical care, sustained categorical efforts will be required to provide effective services to patients with chronic disorders that involve considerable handicap. In doing so, emphasis should be given to interventions that have the highest probability of minimizing disability and reducing suffering. When care is given primarily to comfort and support, priority should be given to patients with the greatest distress and impairment. Interventions should be measured by the degree to which they enhance performance and social functioning (Mechanic 1969).

It is difficult to specify with precision the number of persons in the population who need more intensive services than those likely to be available through the general medical sector. The President's Commission on Mental Health (1977:4) has estimated that as much as 15 percent of the population may need some form of mental-health care at any one time. A more reasonable estimate is that from 10 to 15 percent of the population will at some time in their lives require some level of psychiatric assistance beyond the usual capacity of the primary-care physician. Although for many such patients the need for such care will be a short interlude in their lives, as in the case of many reactive depressions, others—such as schizophrenics, who may constitute between 1 and 2 percent of the population—will require continuing treatment throughout their lives and will consume considerable mental-health resources. Still others, such as those with bipolar depression, alcoholism, and drug addiction, will need, depending on the severity of the problem, periodic treatment. In theory, many of these patients could be cared for in general medical settings, but the practicalities make it unlikely that an adequate pattern of services for such patients can be sustained.

Although some primary-care physicians with an interest in psychiatry may be able to manage chronic patients between episodes of more serious problems, the demands on primary-care facilities make it inevitable that these impaired and frequently difficult patients will be inadequately monitored and neglected. Given the complexity of their problems and the intractability of their conditions, they will frustrate physicians and will suffer stigmatization by both medical and nonmedical personnel. Moreover, these patients require a sustained community approach in addition to whatever medical and drug treatment they receive, and it is unlikely that an unspecialized medical context can effectively organize such services.

Whatever efforts are made to extend mental-health benefits under NHI must not overshadow the needs of the severely impaired patients who require services organized independently of the traditional medical sector. Moreover, such services will have to be provided largely by nonmedical personnel, who may not be covered under NHI. Services for these patients must include diagnosis and assessment, appropriate medical care, sheltered care and preparation for limited employment, aggressive monitoring and training for community living, and continuing social supports. Although a variety of viable models have been developed in demonstration projects (Stein and Test 1978), we have as yet failed to develop any sustained way of financing these efforts on a continuing basis. Even under the best of conditions, such programs are difficult to organize and maintain (Mechanic 1978c). Without financial stability they have little chance to become established.

In sum, we might generally think of patients as having three levels of need, varying from the most prevalent conditions involving only modest interventions to those less frequent but more severe conditions requiring a wide range of medical and social services. The largest group of problems, involving a lack of general well-being and a sense of psychophysiological discomfort, is most properly managed within the general medical sector as a component of comprehensive medical care as well as by nonmedical services. A second category of more disabling conditions, such as depression, alcoholism, and severe neuroses, might best be managed through a collaborative effort

involving the general medical sector but with significant assistance
from psychiatric consultation and community supportive groups.
The most severely impaired patients should receive highest priority
for special categorical services involving medical and psychiatric
assistance, but also the entire spectrum of community care services.

Psychiatric Care under Prepayment Plans

The pattern of insurance benefits that has evolved under fee-for-
service plans has been designed to accommodate to the existing
psychiatry marketplace, which is largely organized around office-
based psychotherapy. Stringent controls on the use of services were
necessary because psychiatrists, particularly those with a psycho-
analytic orientation, would carry out long courses of "treatment" at
great expense with patients who had minimal or no obvious impairment. The effect of paying for such services was to subsidize disproportionately the most affluent and educated groups in the
population, because it was they who were most likely to seek out
psychotherapy, who were most attractive to psychotherapists, and
who were best able to absorb the cost-sharing obligations involved in
the insurance package. Persons of lower income in need of service are
more likely to be inhibited by coinsurance and deductibles.

An alternative model is found in many prepaid practice programs
that maintain greater control over the referral process and the assessment of the need for services. This allows them to provide more
liberal outpatient benefits without the usual cost-sharing deterrents.
Experience in a variety of such plans indicates that outpatient
utilization can be maintained at reasonable levels if the primary
physician plays a gatekeeper role (Follette and Cummings 1967,
1968; Goldberg, Krantz, and Locke 1970; and Fullerton, Lohrenz,
and Nycz 1976). Because these plans involve the primary-care physician's referral, the need for such consent has a moderating effect on
the claim for services. Also, the number of psychiatrists available in
the plan and the queue for service set a natural ceiling on the number
of services that can be consumed and with what intensiveness.
Moreover, when the psychiatrists are themselves employees of the
plan, when they are conscious of the cost implications of utilization,
and when they have no economic incentive to prolong counseling or
psychotherapy, treatment tends to be less intense and to be provided

for shorter periods of time. Also, it is likely that such plans select psychiatric personnel who are more attuned to pragmatic approaches to psychiatric care and to short-term psychotherapy.

From an organizational view, the prepaid plan also offers an advantage in that it facilitates the use of nonmedical personnel in providing mental-health services. Such programs may employ psychologists and social workers and can, therefore, provide services less expensively than programs that depend entirely on psychiatrists. In contrast, most insurance policies reimburse only medical personnel in the fee-for-service sector, creating an unnecessary dependence on the most expensive types of manpower when other mental-health personnel can do as well. Capitation-type plans facilitate the provision of a broader range of services at reasonable cost, are potentially able to make use of the entire spectrum of suitable personnel, and forge a closer alliance between general medical care and more specialized mental-health services.

Although, in theory, the prepaid model offers the most rational and efficient way to handle mental-health problems of the most common types, we know relatively little about how well they do so. The economic feasibility of this model has been demonstrated, but it would be helpful to have a better understanding of the referral decisions made by primary-care physicians, of who obtains and fails to get treatment, and of the quality of mental-health care provided. Although the prepaid organization has an intuitive logic to it, we need more careful study of the way the system really works, the determinants of the referral process, and the outcomes of care relative to alternative approaches.

Critical Issues for National Health Insurance

In recent years private insurance has been extended to a wide range of outpatient services. As part of this trend there has been a cautious growth of psychiatric outpatient coverage. Inpatient psychiatric coverage has improved more rapidly on the reasonable assumption that few persons would frivolously seek psychiatric hospitalization, given the unpleasant nature of the experience and the stigma associated with it. Moreover, the extension of coverage occurred concomitantly with a social movement away from hospital care for psychiatric patients, which mitigated some of the risks involved in providing economic incentives for hospital admissions. Experience to date suggests that the abuse of psychiatric inpatient benefits is not extensive. Such coverage, however, has facilitated a shift in the auspices of care for many patients from public mental hospitals to community voluntary hospitals. Given the inadequacies of the public mental hospitals, this change was beneficial, but before cementing this pattern through NHI, we would do well to examine carefully the adequacy of psychiatric units in general hospitals and the possibility that certain programmatic standards should be mandated to achieve eligibility for reimbursement under NHI. These units seem to vary a great deal from the innovative to the unimaginative. Many of these units are modeled on the medical perspective and lack adequate therapeutic and activity programs that maintain the patient's involvement. In some of these units patients spend their days with no more activity than was found in custodial mental hospitals. These psychiatric units frequently forgo excellent opportunities for rehabilitative programs by copying a pattern of service more suitable for a medical or surgical ward.

The extension of private insurance has had little direct impact on the public mental-health sector because public institutions that do not collect fees from uninsured patients are usually not reimbursed for care by private insurers. The future extension of psychiatric inpatient benefits to all citizens under NHI, however, provides a potential opportunity to upgrade all mental-health services. NHI would increase the flow of patients away from public mental hospitals to voluntary hospitals, and some hope that NHI will further the disappearance of the public mental hospital. The reduction of patient demand in public mental hospitals, however, might assist in upgrading services for those who remain. To the extent that public hospitals compete with voluntary hospitals successfully in some communities because of unique programs or because of accessibility to particular populations, they should be allowed to recoup reimbursement without penalty. It is not clear, however, how state governments can be induced to avoid using new sources of funds as replacements for state appropriations when faced with fiscal pressures.

Although it is unlikely that many patients would seek out psychiatric hospitalization when it is unnecessary, psychiatrists tend to have a great deal of control over hospitalization decisions. At the margin, it is the ideology of the psychiatrist and the incentives affecting his behavior that will determine the rate of hospital use. Depending on the mix of inpatient and outpatient benefits, it is conceivable that NHI could provide incentives for psychiatrists to hospitalize patients more readily than desirable. Although the profession has been active in developing utilization-review criteria, it is difficult to see how peer review could effectively police varying discretionary decisions in the middle range. The basis for much psychiatric decision making is vague and easily manipulatable by the manner in which the attending psychiatrist chooses to describe the case.

There is a serious danger that NHI will create the illusion that the needs of psychiatric patients are being dealt with, thus reducing pressures for continued and increased funding to develop a community network of rehabilitative and supportive services. By extending hospital coverage for the entire population, NHI may promote a traditional medical response when what is most needed for the chronic population is a sustained pattern of community services for those facing a long life with impairments in work, interpersonal relationships, and ordinary social functioning. As the NHI discussion focuses on which of various professionals will be reimbursed as mental-health providers and on what basis, the interests of the most severely impaired patients are not well represented. One possible approach would be to develop a mental-health resource fund that would constitute some fraction of all psychiatric benefits provided under NHI. This fund could be used for grants to develop community networks of care and support for deinstitutionalized patients and could be specifically earmarked for programs involving other than personal psychiatric services. A development fund for mental-health resources is one mechanism to develop greater equity in the system for the chronic patient.

In this chapter emphasis has been given to two groups of patients who have ordinarily been outside the mainstream in planning for psychiatric care. The first group, involving those with the least-handicapping problems, can probably be served most efficiently by improvements in the primary-medical-care sector. The second group, chronic mental patients, requires concerted and sustained efforts to ensure their integration into community life at a tolerable level of functioning. What evidence do we have that this can be achieved?

There is some indication that providing responsive mental-health care to chronically complaining medical patients results in an overall reduction in medical and hospital utilization (Follette and Cummings 1967). Because such patients are often exposed to repeated and expensive diagnostic care to assess their vague symptoms and treatment to deal with their persistent complaints of discomfort, attention to mental-health problems may turn out to be the most cost-effective pattern of care. Demonstration programs in prepaid practices have shown that it is economically feasible to provide such care, at least in controlled settings, and this appears to be the most humane alternative. However, many patients resist mental-health definitions, and, thus, such care must be provided in a subtle and unobtrusive way. There is evidence that careful instructions for patients that provide coping alternatives and that are psychologically and culturally credible are constructive in helping them face threatening and anxiety-provoking situations (Mechanic 1972c; Leventhal 1970).

In the case of the chronically ill there is unequivocal experience indicating that existing psychiatric treatment itself without a carefully designed system of supportive services cannot cope with the dimensions of the patients' problems or the social costs assumed by the community (Stein and Test 1976; Davis, Dinitz, and Pasamanick 1972). No system of psychiatric insurance coverage can meet these patients' needs without resources and efforts to design programs to keep patients involved and in contact, working to the extent feasible, and associating with other people and continuing-care programs. To treat these patients episodically and return them to a community without adequate programming displaces the problems without providing the instruments necessary to deal with them.

NHI provides opportunities for improving the care of all the mentally ill, but only if those forces concerned with the long-term chronic patients represent their needs in the hard bargaining that is inevitable in hammering out a major new social program.

IV | Social Regulation of Medical Care

8

Theories of Rationing

When methods of production are too expensive to provide for all the services defined as necessary, and when patient demand is too large in relation to the resources available, then care must be distributed on the basis of some allocative principle. The severity of rationing required depends on (1) the ability to produce services more economically or to develop functional substitutes; (2) the effectiveness in reducing demand by preventing illness, limiting the domain of responsibility of medical care, or changing consumers' expectations of and desire for care; and (3) the aggregate resources that individuals and government are willing to invest in medical care at any point in time.

There is no scientific way of determining how much a society ought to invest in medical care in relation to other needs and desires. Such outcomes depend on tastes, values, and economic and political factors. Moreover, the issue is particularly difficult to resolve when individuals are insulated from appreciating the real magnitude of cost financed through third-party payment, government programs, and collectively won fringe benefits. Also, when the expenditure pattern is constructed on the basis of hundreds of thousands of individual decisions, rather than a collective judgment, there is no way to impose an orderly set of priorities.

The Market as an Allocative Mechanism

The growth of third-party payment and government responsibility for health care is a relatively recent phenomenon in the United States, and throughout much of the world medical care is still

91

available only to those who can purchase it. In the traditional pattern of medicine, those with financial means could command whatever level of medical care was available, while those without means were dependent for care on the beneficence of government, philanthropists, the church, or physicians themselves. Because affluence was limited, and medical technology and knowledge in any case offered only modest gains, the market served as a way of distributing the limited range of services that did exist. While the church, philanthropists, and government all established hospitals for the sick who had no other place to be, the early hospitals were more refuges than treatment institutions, and patients with any means avoided them and received their care at home.

The market as an effective allocative mechanism broke down as a result of a variety of social forces. First, medical knowledge and technology expanded rapidly, increasing patients' desires and demands for a wide range of medical services. The hospital, which was formerly a refuge for the destitute, evolved into the central locus of scientific medical practice. As technology developed, the costs of caring for a serious medical episode very much increased and imposed on the ill a financial burden that was large and unpredictable. The population increasingly sought means of sharing such risks through benevolent societies and insurance plans, and as costs mounted, consumers demanded that government assume a growing proportion of these expenditures. Thus, what was primarily a fee-for-service sector shifted to one dominated by a variety of third-party payment. In the late nineteenth and early twentieth centuries government programs for medical care began to emerge in Europe, consolidating the efforts of many voluntary societies, while in the United States the demand for the protection of risk against serious and expensive illness resulted first in the development of voluntary insurance as a means of neutralizing the pressure for a nationalized health system, and later in a variety of government medical-care programs to subsidize care of the poor, the old, the disabled, and other categorical groups.

Cost Sharing as a Means of Rationing

Even under the most favorable circumstances the medical marketplace had many imperfections as a method of allocating scarce resources (Arrow 1963; Klarman 1965; Mechanic 1978b). With the growth of third-party payment, however, there were few incentives for either patients or providers to conserve resources because neither were penalized by excessive utilization. As the insurance sector grew, the marketplace more blatantly failed as an effective mode of allocation, but some of its features have persisted. One such cost-sharing feature—coinsurance and deductibles—remains as a rationing device on the assumption that if consumers must share in the costs of their care they may use services more wisely, and, even if they do not, they will at least be held responsible for part of the total cost, thus reducing financial pressures on insurers or government. Although cost sharing probably has such effects, like the marketplace as a whole, it places different inhibitions on the poor than on those more affluent. Further, cost barriers have a larger effect on the use of ambulatory care or medications than on more expensive services under the physician's control. While it is argued that when patients must pay part of their hospital-care costs they are more likely to pressure the physician for early release as well as other economies, this is more conjecture than demonstrated fact.

The use of cost sharing as a means of rationing raises a variety of issues for which more data are required. First, to what extent does cost sharing affect the utilization of different types of services and procedures? Second, in respect to procedures under the control of physicians, such as hospitalization and surgical intervention, to what extent do patients actually influence physicians as a result of cost-sharing pressures? Third, to what extent are physicians aware of the coinsurance and deductible provisions of their patients' insurance policies and, if they are, how does it affect their behavior? Although economists differ in estimations of the elasticities of medical-care consumption, it is clear that cost-sharing provisions affect consumption of services under the control of patients more substantially than those under the control of the physician. Effects are particularly large for use of ambulatory services, psychiatric services, dental services, and so on. The size of the effects differs depending on the specific cost-sharing arrangements and on the economic status of the persons involved. Cost sharing differentially affects the poor as compared with the affluent and results in equalities in the distribution of medical care.

Although there are no studies directly dealing with the assumption that cost sharing leads patients to influence physician behavior, it seems plausible that this occurs to some degree. Existing studies suggest, however, that physicians are not well informed on the scope of insurance coverage of their patients, and studies of consumers indicate as well that they, too, frequently lack detailed knowledge of the provisions of their health insurance. Although patients may become better informed about their coverage when such issues become salient for them, existing experience does not provide much confidence that physicians are substantially influenced by patients' insurance coverage. It was widely believed that expansion of benefits to the ambulatory context would reduce waste because physicians would do in their offices many of the procedures formerly done in hospitals, but empirical studies demonstrate that extending the range of benefits without other controls results in large increases in use of ambulatory care and small increases in hospital care as well (Lewis and Keairnes 1970).

   Cost sharing as a rationing device is often opposed because of its differential effects on persons of varying incomes, because it is believed to create barriers to necessary care, and because administration of such mechanisms is costly. Those advocating such rationing seem to believe that patients are sufficiently knowledgeable to differentiate serious from trivial symptoms, and that a cost-sharing mechanism encourages them to make such distinctions. Although there are certainly instances in which this applies, studies of illness behavior of patient populations suggest that decisions to seek care are influenced by factors other than those viewed by physicians as most important from a medical standpoint. Patients give more attention to symptoms that disrupt ordinary activities and routines than to those that may pose greater potential threat but are more innocuous (Mechanic 1978a:279- 80). The assumption that patients who are worried and fearful can and should make judgments of the medical significance of their symptoms is inconsistent with the notion that a major function of the physician is to make judgments concerning the significance of symptoms. In retrospect, many patients' complaints are trivial, but often what the patient seeks is reassurance from the physician that this is the case and relief from uncertainty and anxiety. It is strange to hear, on the one hand, that the ordinary patient is in a good position to make such judgments and, on the other, that only a physician with eight or ten years of medical training can effectively deliver first-contact care.

   If patients can make wise decisions about when care is necessary, then one would anticipate that cost sharing would result in a different mix of services, because patients who are seriously ill would be more likely to seek care. The fragmentary data that exist on this issue suggest that cost-sharing provisions have an overall rationing effect with impact on both "trivial" and serious categories of utilization. For example, increases in the prescription charge in the national health service affect not only drugs used primarily as placebos but also drug maintenance for serious chronic illness. Even without cost barriers, it is difficult to maintain surveillance and adherence to therapy among persons who have serious medical conditions. Although patients respond primarily to the way symptoms affect their experience, the role of the physician is to assess the implications of particular symptoms for a person's future health status. The fact that physicians often engage in expensive diagnostic appraisal of ordinary symptoms suggests that the evaluation of their clinical significance may not be as simple as cost-sharing advocates imply. It seems, therefore, that if more stringent rationing is to be applied, it is applied more rationally in relation to those who have most expertise and knowledge and who are in a better position to differentiate the serious from the trivial.

Implicit and Explicit Rationing

To the extent that the marketplace is rejected as a means of rationing care, and as cost-sharing measures erode because of public opposition to them, other alternatives must be developed for allocating health-care services to the population. As already suggested, rationing occurs by influencing the behavior of the patient, the physician, or the administrative structure of the medical-care plan. In addition to fee barriers, other rationing measures may be imposed on consumers, such as increased waiting times and other inconveniences, limited access to specialized services through required referral from primary physicians, increased distances to sites of care or restricted hours of services, and a variety of bureaucratic barriers. Most such barriers naturally occur when demand for service exceeds availability, but they are undesirable if they seriously limit access to care among patients in need.

A second type of rationing places barriers on the physician by limiting the resources available—what I have called implicit rationing. Such rationing is implicit in the sense that the physician's rationing decisions are not specified but rather depend on his clinical judgment. For example, capitation payment requires the physician to decide how to allocate his time and resources among patients for whom he is responsible. Unlike the present situation, in which the doctor can draw on insurance resources in an open-ended way to provide services and perform procedures, implicit rationing sets a limit on what the physician can do. Similarly, implicit rationing refers to limitations in resources as exemplified by fixed prospective budgets, limitations on available beds, and fixed numbers of specialists in certain areas. The National Health Service of England and health-maintenance organizations are typical examples of implicit rationing.

Explicit rationing, in contrast, refers to direct administrative decisions affecting the provision of care involving inclusions and exclusions of coverage within health-care plans or in respect to particular subpopulations, limitations on the availability of specific types of visits or procedures, required prior review for performing certain procedures, utilization review, and required intervals between the provision of certain services. Explicit rationing involves the transfer of certain decisions from the professional's discretion to a more centralized administrative process. All health-care systems use some mix of market, implicit, and explicit rationing to allocate available services to the population. The challenge is to identify the mix most appropriate for satisfying social goals at an acceptable cost.

All theories of rationing imply models of human behavior that, if incorrect, lead to faulty expectations as to their actual performance in practice. For example, there have been a variety of incentive reimbursement programs developed in recent years designed to encourage hospital administrators to use resources more efficiently. The assumption of these programs has been that if you make it advantageous for the administrator to seek economies, he will do so. What is not clear, however, is that administrators—even if they are motivated—are in a position to bring about many of the changes desired. Decision-making powers are widely dispersed in hospitals, and cost problems are substantially associated with the decisions of individual physicians who use the institution as their work place. Administrators are often in a weak position in relation to the medical staff, who question the administrator's authority to interfere in clinical judgments, and the administrator is not necessarily in control of many of the hospital's ancillary services. Thus it should be no great surprise that incentive reimbursement programs thus far have been disappointing in their impact on hospital cost (Reinholds

1976:24– 25). If such programs are to be effective in the future, a much better understanding of the behavioral system of medical institutions, physicians, and patients is necessary (Mechanic 1976a).

Consider, for example, the assumption that when professionals face resource limitations they are encouraged to make sound clinical judgments on the priority of need and efficiency of intervention. It is commonly assumed that fixed budgets require professionals to examine their decisions more carefully and that they result in physicians treating illness early to avoid further morbidity and greater future medical-care costs. Underlying this assumption is the belief that physicians are adequately "programmed" by their training to make scientifically valid judgments of need and priority of need; that they will be motivated to act ethically and to take whatever measures are best for their patients as opposed to other interests; and that, because of their proximity to the contingencies of care, they are in the best position to make decisions about priorities.

Although these assumptions seem reasonable on the face of it, there are a variety of contingencies of medical practice that make them less powerful than they may appear. First, medical practice is characterized by considerable uncertainty as to the amount of care necessary for many problems, and the relationships between most processes of care and outcomes are at best ambiguous. Thus the clinician's judgments in such matters are less likely to reflect any rigorous criteria of effectiveness than they are likely to reflect his or her training and style of practice, which serve as a weak basis on which to make rationing judgments. Second, physicians engage in complex and subtle interactions with patients that affect both patient response and physician behavior. Physicians find it difficult to refuse services demanded by more sophisticated, knowledgeable, and educated patients, and such refusal is made even more risky because the standards themselves are so vague and physicians may lack confidence in their own rationing criteria. Physicians, thus, are more likely to ride with the tide, rationing more stringently when there are no protests from patients but being somewhat more liberal in use of resources when patients expect and demand this (Hetherington, Hopkins, and Roemer 1975). The problem is that the more sophisticated and aggressive patients receive disproportionate services while those who are less educated and more passive may receive fewer services despite the fact that they have more illness and greater need.

Further, the assumption that implicit rationing allows physicians to make more professional decisions because it separates their profes-

sional judgments from fee considerations, while plausible, is a weak
assumption. Physicians are influenced in many ways by their training, personal needs, and desire for prestige and recognition. The fact
that fee considerations are no longer relevant does not ensure that
the physician will not be influenced by personal agendas and professional preferences. In the absence of economic incentives they may
work at a more comfortable and leisurely pace, devote less time to
their patients, give disproportionate time to more interesting and
prestigious tasks, and generally organize their schedules to offer a
more stimulating and attractive day. As previously noted, there is
evidence that when capitation is the primary mode of payment,
physicians devote fewer hours to their patients than fee-for-service
physicians, refer patients to other types of facilities more readily,
and may be more inflexible and less responsive in dealing with
patients (Mechanic 1976a). In short, implicit rationing by itself,
without carefully worked out incentives affecting remuneration,
recognition, and peer evaluation, provides no assurance of good
allocations of limited resources or equitable results.

The fact is that we lack detailed understanding of the behavioral
factors affecting the decisions of individual physicians, and each
physician recognizes the legitimacy of interference in his clinical
responsibilities only to a very limited extent. As Freidson notes in a
careful study of one large prepaid group practice,

> the subordinates of the medical group, the working physicians, were in-
> clined to concede legitimacy to the exercise of administrative authority in
> only extremely limited areas of their work. There was no real issue of
> recognizing the *formal* legitimacy of such authority. The issue was, rather,
> willingness to accept the systematic and regular exercise of that authority
> over the whole range of their work [Freidson 1975:118].

Developing incentives within capitation systems for both efficient and high-quality care is a tricky problem. The development of
such incentives must take into account not only the uncertainty of
practice and the ease with which formal procedures can be thwarted,
but also the training and ideology of the physicians, the pattern of
peer influences, which is now relatively weak, and the situational
contingencies likely to affect performance, such as work load, availability of ancillary assistance, and patient mix. The difficulty of
achieving any effective direct control over professional decision
making is one argument for an administrative approach to rationing.
Explicit rationing is such an approach.

The use of explicit rationing techniques has been based on a variety of beliefs. First, it has been assumed that when governments or administrators assume more centralized control over the allocation of health funds and the establishment of priorities among varying health-care options, a more equitable distribution of resources is likely to occur than through either fee-for-service or implicit rationing techniques. Through more centralized control it is theoretically possible to assign funds in relationship to ascertained need of particular population groups, to apportion resources more fairly among varying geographic areas, and to establish areas of health-care investment with higher benefit-cost outcomes. Second, it is assumed that aggregate data available to administrators, and the results of careful studies and controlled clinical trials when they exist, serve as a better basis for allocation decisions than the individual judgments of practitioners, who may work from clinical impressions and experiences that lack any scientific basis. Third, explicit rationing in part takes the burden of rationing out of the hands of the physician, thus alleviating conflicts of interest inherent in the doctor-patient relationship in which the physician has major responsibility for denying patients services. Moreover, explicit rationing puts the onus of rationing on an outside administrative authority, which may prevent physician-patient conflicts and reduce stresses in clinical relationships.

As to the first assumption, it is correct, at least in principle, that planning authorities can decide on such issues as total expenditures, the allocation of resources among varying population groups, the appropriate mix between physicians and other types of health personnel, and the relative distribution of resources between primary- and secondary-care levels. Moreover, administrators can exclude payment for procedures that are likely to yield low benefits or that are of high risk relative to their benefits, or they can specify when or by whom such procedures can be performed by requiring prior review or by specifying necessary credentials for eligibility for reimbursement. The conception of this planning process, however, is excessively rational and fails to take into account the susceptibility of these processes to political influences or public pressures. Even the most cursory examination of health planning would provide a sobering demonstration that there is a wide gap between rational planning and political outcomes.

There is little evidence to support the belief that explicit rationing per se will result in a fairer allocation of resources. Indeed, problems of redistribution in the medical sector are probably in many ways similar to income redistribution more generally, and are subject to many of the same kinds of political pressures. Such redistribution is probably most feasible when resources are expanding and extraordinarily difficult in a relatively stable situation. If we examine the English National Health Service, in which there has been a strong redistribution ideology among the Labor government and in which budget making in health is relatively insulated from public pressures as compared with the United States, it is still clear that there has been only modest redistribution (Logan 1971; Cooper 1975). Large disparities persist in the availability of resources by geography and in per capita expenditures for manpower and resources. Moreover, there continues to be large variation from area to area, and from one institution to another, in levels of technology, work load, and staffing. New efforts are now being made to redistribute resources, with great resistance among the more affluent hospitals. Also, when funds are made available on a theoretically equal basis, as in the Medicare program in the United States, large inequalities result from varying availability of physicians and facilities (Davis 1975).

Problems exist as well in respect to the quality of administrative decision making. Although, in theory, allocation decisions made on an aggregate data base are probably better than individual clinical judgments, the fact is that in many areas adequate data are not likely to be available in a form allowing firm decisions to be made. Although it is useful to talk about controlled clinical trials, investigations relating process to outcome, and cost-benefit studies, good investigations of these types are the exception rather than the rule and are difficult to carry out. Much of medical practice will remain uncertain for the foreseeable future and not easily subsumed under formally prescribed guidelines. The problems of patients and types of medical facilities serving them are highly varied and complex, and it is very unlikely that effective guidelines can be written to cover these situations without creating a host of new problems. Thus although standards may be formulated effectively for some situations, medical practice in general will continue to require a great deal of professional discretion.

Another problem with explicit rationing is that those who develop regulations and guidelines are often divorced from the complex contingencies of everyday practice, the variabilities from one context to another, and the kind of sensitivity that comes from working with the problems themselves. In attempting to devise general principles for different settings, a variety of injustices and absurdities may result. This may in part be prevented by a sensitive process of review and commentary on proposed regulations, but even under the best of circumstances standard rules fail to cover adequately contingencies likely to occur at the service level.

With explicit rationing physicians are insulated from the charge that they are promoting their own interests against those of patients. Problems of this sort are increasingly likely with the types of incentive systems that provide bonuses to physicians for cost-effective practice and that require them to share losses when there are cost overruns. Within a pure explicit rationing system, physicians can still advocate doing everything possible for patients, serving as the patients' representative in relation to the plan. To the extent that there are limits on the services available, it is the system that does not provide them rather than the physician who denies them. This protects the patient–physician relationship from suspicion and hostility, which may become more common in systems requiring physicians to play a strict rationing role. It has been suggested that to put the physician into this position is unethical because it undermines and dilutes primary responsibility to the patient (Fried 1975). The contending argument is that physicians, because of their accessibility to the complexity of the individual case, may be in a better position than an administrator to make a reasonable judgment of what is demanded by the patient's clinical situation.

The Role of the Public in Establishing Rationing Priorities

Whatever the approach to rationing, both the mechanisms used and the consequences must achieve public legitimacy. To the extent that the public perceives favoritism, cheating, or other violations of the expected allocative processes, considerable problems are likely to develop. The definition of an equitable allocative process depends on the values and perceptions of the population, but these are not easily ascertained. Some data are available from opinion polls, but the answers depend to a considerable degree on the way the questions and alternatives are posed. One can observe the behavior of politicians, who at least in theory represent the value choices of the population, but this does not provide a very specific sense of what the public desires and thus can be misleading. It might be possible to put together on the basis of existing data a model that specifies what the public would wish, assuming that it had full information on needs, the true costs and benefits of medical care, and the existing distribution of care, but this would be no simple task.

The population is an amorphous collection of individuals and groups having varying interests, information, experience, and understanding of human problems. Some feel deeply about social problems and others remain apathetic. Even if we knew how to pose the precise questions, it is not clear that we would know how to weigh the responses, taking into account that medical care has different degrees of importance to individuals. Even more difficult is communicating to the public in a fashion it can understand the nature of the policy issues required for meaningful decisions. To have statistical information is quite different from really appreciating the experience of others in a situation of unfulfilled need. This is the stuff that novels and theater are made of, but it is as real as the statistics themselves. People distant from events can psychologically remove themselves, and their judgments under such conditions are quite different from those they would have if they came face to face with the problem (Milgram 1974). Can a person who has never seen a schizophrenic or a psychotically depressed patient really appreciate what it means to have such a patient in a family setting? The more distant the experience, the more difficult it is to empathize with those hypothetical people who have the problem.

Public-interest lawyers who wish to obtain judicial decisions in favor of the mentally ill will often attempt to have the judge visit the institutions concerned. They know that the stark reality is very different from the hypothetical, and that emotional appreciation is different from cognitive understanding. In public discussion of numerous public policies involving an almost infinite number of situations, it is extraordinarily difficult to achieve public appreciation of the real problem unless it is sufficiently prevalent that the average person has had some contact with it. In such areas as heart disease and cancer, with which most families have had some contact through relatives or friends who had the problem, it is relatively easy to elicit public support. Similarly, some organizations devoted to less prevalent conditions—such as the National Kidney Foundation—are remarkably successful in exploiting public media and eliciting attention. There are many areas of health and disease, however, in which the public has only the vaguest appreciation of needs and what the illness involves, but unless such appreciation is part of the decision-making process, seemingly rational decisions can be extraordinarily insensitive.

The foregoing pertains to the views of experts as well as the general public. In such fields as economics, operations research, and the management sciences, planning tools may be applied that reveal only very superficial appreciation of the experiential aspects of the problem or the human dimensions of the area being addressed. Although distance may provide a wider, and some say "more objective," field of vision, it may also contribute to a callousness that might not occur if the planner saw the problem as the patient, the family, and the therapist have to see it. We all become hardened to abstract difficulties. Perhaps this is necessary for psychological survival. In defending ourselves against pain, however, we must guard against so losing perspective that we contribute to its exacerbation.

9 | Patients' Rights and the
Regulation of Medical Practice

In the previous chapter various means for controlling physicians' behavior were discussed, but with a focus on cost control. Problems of cost containment are creating great pressures to use resources more efficiently, to ration services, and to avoid duplication of facilities. Among the mechanisms being advocated are fixed prospective budgeting, capitation payment, regionalization of facilities, and control over the development of new facilities. Although these measures may all have value in promoting important national goals and in conserving scarce resources, if successful they inevitably restrict the choices available to consumers of medical care, their ability to select services in a "marketplace," and their ability to exercise control over the professionals and institutions that serve them.

Medical care, however, is most basically a relationship between patients and professionals, and the quality of care depends on the effectiveness of their communication. The relationship has increasingly become complicated as a result of more elaborate technology, the wide array of personnel who play some part in the care process, increased bureaucratization of medical services, and more complex financing arrangements. Although tightening the organization and provision of medical services may be a rational way of using expensive national resources, attention must be given to the protection of patients' rights and the accountability of the health professionals who serve them. The purpose of this chapter is to discuss ethical problems that arise in rationing medical care, and in medical practice more generally, and possible approaches to minimizing such problems without excessive regulatory costs.

In the past twenty years there has developed a significant aware-

104

ness and sensitivity to human rights in such varied areas as employment practices, education, and research. Considerable progress has been made in defining ethical issues and the relationships between the rights of persons and the powers of the institutions that affect them. Physicians greatly value their autonomy and are an extraordinarily powerful group, and the practice of medicine has remained relatively immune to developments that have affected the ways other social institutions operate. There is, however, evidence of dissatisfaction with medical care and of increasing distrust of physicians and other health providers. Trust is further eroded by growing impersonality of care and by feelings on the part of patients that they have no control over a vital institution that affects their lives. Increasingly we hear that physicians, other health professionals, and medical institutions should be held more accountable.

There are innumerable ethical problems inherent in patient care as there are in any complex human relationship in which there are inequities in power and dependence between the persons involved. Given the vast differences in knowledge between the typical physician and patient and the exaggerated dependency associated with illness, patients are in a position in which they must trust the wisdom and integrity of those who care for them. There are many potential violations of such trust, but to enumerate them or attempt to devise specific rules to prevent them is largely an exercise in futility. Most rules are easily subverted in practice; when regulations are imposed, efforts are often devoted to meeting their bureaucratic requirements without major impact on behavior; and the proliferation of regulation itself adversely affects morale and practice. Thus, in considering imposing possible controls on the service sector, it is necessary to weigh the magnitude of the problems and the likely gains achieved through regulation against the costs of imposing further bureaucratic rules. Health care is provided under real constraints of time, manpower, and resources, and controls add to the costs of service and the burdens on health-care personnel. Time devoted to monitoring and enforcement of specific rules and affirmations of compliance is time taken from other valued activities, and regulation may be counterproductive in its consequences. The imposition of any regulation thus should be evaluated not only in terms of its expected symbolic and practical benefits in changing behavior, reaffirming essential values, and reassuring the public but also in terms of its real costs in diverting professional energies and resources from other important activities, discouraging innovation and creativity through incentives for safe bureaucratic response, and eroding morale.

Although the identification of problems usually elicits the response that "there ought to be a rule," such rule making designed to constrain behavior or to punish violators is negative in its approach and does little to increase sensitivity or educational dialogue. Effective guidelines in an area as vast and complex as medical care would contribute to informing professionals and others of problems they may be unaware of and to making them more cognizant of and sensitive to the strong feelings and views of others. In short, good regulation contains a strong educational component.

Ethical Principles in Service Delivery

Medical practice has the potential for many ethical dilemmas. They range from such everyday concerns as the ways physicians communicate to patients, inform them about their illnesses, and explain options to profound decisions concerning the prolongation or termination of life. Moreover, these issues exist at every level of practice and administration, from the individual decisions of the physician to the formulation of global health policy. Notions of health and illness, types of financing, mechanisms for remuneration, the concept of a medical-care service, the definition of practitioners eligible for payment—all of these come to shape the delivery of services and their impact on patients' lives. The decision of policy-makers, for example, to pay for hemodialysis, hip replacements, and other technical procedures for the aged, but not for social care, counseling, or homemaker services, has major impact on the life opportunities of the old for independent living and involves important ethical issues.

In this discussion I take as my primary ethical principle the fundamental notion of respect for every person. I use the term "respect" to refer to lack of partiality or discrimination, and in this sense the concept is different from esteem or veneration. Although the concept itself is open to varying interpretations, any use of it is based on four derivatives for which there is a broad social consensus:

    a. All patients should be free of coercion, participating in medical-care, research, and educational programs only with their informed consent.

b. Every patient should receive accurate factual information, to the extent possible, pertaining to his or her care, risks involved, and rights in the medical context.

c. Within whatever economic limitations are operative, decisions concerning medical care should be made solely on the basis of medical need and expected medical benefits, and not on social, political, or religious criteria.

d. When conflicts develop between patients and providers, mechanisms should be available for a fair resolution.

Sources of Ethical Problems in Health-Care Delivery: Definition of the Problem

Ethical problems in service delivery arise from a variety of sources: (1) inappropriate and unprofessional behavior of providers; (2) limitations on resources relative to demand and resulting rationing pressures; (3) conflicts in values, expectations, and incentives within varying health-delivery plans; and (4) inequalities between health providers and patients.

Professional Behavior of Providers

Health professionals include persons with a wide range of human characteristics as in other comparable occupational groups. It is no surprise that patients sometimes encounter such professionals who demonstrate a lack of respect for them. Nor is the medical context free from manifest and more subtle forms of prejudice and discrimination. The behavior of health-care professionals may vary from one situation to another or from one day to another, reflecting the health professional's personality, mood, or situational stresses or particular characteristics of difficult patients. To the extent that problems arise from such factors or those associated with the personal style of the health professional, they are not easily modified. To the extent that more serious abuses arise because the health professional suffers from a mental illness or serious personality disorder, or because he blatantly violates the trust of his position, clearer options are available. For the most part, however, patients are relatively powerless in the face of professional behavior that is inappropriate or in poor taste.

In theory, unethical professional behavior is contained through careful recruitment and selection of health professionals, through a long period of training and apprenticeship, during which the trainee is socialized in respect to important values as well as in respect to relevant skills, and through review and supervision of performance. The fact is, however, that the long period of medical training socializes the physician to a distinctive point of view, one very different from the views of the typical patient. There are a variety of formal and informal mechanisms that exist in medical practice to detect significant departures: medical-practice committees, boards, and tissue committees. Too much confidence is placed, however, in the existing peer-review structure as a means of preventing violations of ethical principles. Nor is the value of professional standards review organizations, mandatory continuing education, or periodic relicensing as promising as some would hope. The tradition of exclusive self-regulation by medicine has served more to insulate the profession from outside influence than to protect the rights of patients (Freidson 1970b). Even with the best of intentions, doctors have a different perspective than patients and may have difficulty understanding the patient's point of view. With the exception of serious mental illness, alcoholism or drug addiction, or criminal behavior, suspensions or revocations of licenses or other serious sanctions are rare. There are few alternatives to the more drastic sanctions, such as suspension of license, and this is a deterrent to applying any sanctions at all.

There is little willingness among physicians to control or sanction one another and some evidence that physicians with similar behavioral tendencies associate with one another (Freidson 1970a). Although physicians may withhold referrals to and employment from colleagues whose ethical behavior they question, such exclusion does not limit or affect in any significant way the continuation of ethical violations. Moreover, the effectiveness of long medical training as a screening device is an illusion. While medical schools attract applicants with a high level of academic competence, retention rates are extraordinarily high compared with most other types of graduate or postgraduate training and ensure little "weeding out" of undesirable candidates. Similarly, although supervision and negative appraisal during internship or residency may affect the ability of the candidate to obtain the most desirable positions, such supervision and evaluation almost never exclude the candidate from medical employment. In short, the image of a highly selective screening process that ensures quality and ethicality is a mirage, protecting the autonomy of the profession more than the public.

Regulation of autonomous and prestigious professionals is extraordinarily difficult to achieve without producing undesirable side effects. Moreover, in regulating the segment of the profession most likely to engage in violations, burdens are placed inevitably on those who practice a high standard of quality and ethicality in a way that detracts from their performance. These facts support the argument that checks on professional abuses are needed but excessive intrusiveness should be avoided.

Limitation of Resources Relative to Demand: Rationing of Medical Care

Many violations of the principle of respect for persons arise because demand for services is large and resources are limited. Under such conditions services may not be available, and when they are available care becomes rushed, relationships between health professionals and patients become impersonal, and communications, explanations, and opportunities for asking questions and obtaining feedback are more limited. These problems are more likely to occur in relation to minority-group patients or patients in lower socioeconomic circumstances because they are more likely to participate in programs that ration care strictly, while the affluent more frequently participate in programs characterized by open-ended budgeting that have greater availability of personnel and other resources. Even when payment for care is available, as in Medicare or Medicaid, the poor are more likely to reside in areas with lesser concentration of facilities and manpower, making it more difficult for them in "cash in" on their entitlements (Davis 1975).

Many public programs of health care cover certain benefits but rarely provide the necessary resources to meet all eligible needs in the population. The limited resources appropriated by public programs or available in private programs with fixed budgets set the stage for rationing, but the fact that rationing occurs is rarely explicit, and the rules that apply are almost never specified. Because resources are in limited supply, no consumer has an absolute right to services in general; he does, however, have a right to an allocation process that is just and that respects his person (by telling the truth) (Friedman 1969; 1971). More specifically, this requires that the fact that rationing occurs and the way it occurs is generally known, and that it is based on reasonable categorization.

The Concept of Just Rationing. Justice in rationing implies that persons who fit certain criteria be treated equally in respect to the relevant class of services. There is wide agreement that in rationing services the criteria applied should be medical. Determinations of who is to receive priority should be based on need and expected benefits and not on sociocultural or political criteria. Justice in allocation further implies that available services will be distributed so as not to impose an unfair burden on individuals because of their social status, religious or racial background, or personal characteristics unrelated to medical judgments.

The exclusion of payment for abortion under government-sponsored programs, for example, substitutes political and religious considerations for medical judgments. Although exclusion of certain benefits under federal or state programs would be ethically permissible because of resource limitations or because the procedures involved are known to be worthless or harmful, there is no ethical justification for singling out recipients of government programs as ineligible for services known to have positive health benefits that are available to others in the population and that have a high benefit ratio relative to costs. The arbitrary exclusion of abortion under Title 19, or under any other federal or state program, introduces political and religious rationing as a substitute for medical rationing. Moreover, it establishes two standards of access to a positive health benefit (for an objective review of the evidence on the health effects of abortion, see Institute of Medicine 1975), one for government recipients and another for persons in the nongovernmental sector. Such administrative action is a serious violation of the ethical principle that *available medical resources should be equitably administered in relationship to need and expected medical benefit.*

Services may be rationed poorly for reasons other than discrimination. Needy recipients frequently are less educated, less sophisticated, and less aggressive in demanding available services in both public and private programs, while those with greater skills but less need may overcome bureaucratic barriers more readily (Hetherington, Hopkins, and Roemer 1975:127, 135, 281, 292). Non-fee-rationing devices can have inequitable effects in very much the same way as economic barriers (Mechanic 1976a:87–97). Unless concerted efforts are made to ration equitably, those with greater skills and with more worldly sophistication will command a disproportionate share of resources regardless of the rationing techniques used.

At the service level, persons of varying social status may receive different benefits not because of need but because of individual attributes unrelated to the provision of medical care. Although we have no evidence that discrimination systematically occurs, it is frequently alleged that nonwhites, the poor, women, and Title 19 recipients are at risk. These impressions may stem, however, less from discrimination in the provision of services and more from problems in communication, differences in behavioral patterns surrounding illness in varying social and cultural groups, and resulting misunderstandings (Strauss 1969; also see Mechanic 1972a:80–101). Finally, it has been observed that certain categories of patients are treated differently on the basis of social criteria as compared with medical need. For example, it has been alleged that lesser efforts are made to resuscitate alcoholics (Sudnow 1967:100–105), and that services are less available to other patients with stigmatized social identities (Lasagna 1970).

Rationing and Truth Telling. In introducing new programs there tends to be considerable exaggeration as to the benefits to be expected. Such rhetoric raises expectations that are not fulfilled. The marketing of new types of medical-care plans, such as health-maintenance organizations, is an example. When such plans are marketed, they usually promise a comprehensive benefit package, although there is often in reality a reluctance to provide some of the benefits advertised. Enrollment in an HMO is really an agreement between the enrollee and the plan to accept a situation of "constructive rationing," although such plans are rarely described to consumers in this way. For a lower premium, more comprehensive benefits, or both, the consumer implicitly agrees to accept the plan's judgment as to what services are necessary. The nature of this agreement is not usually made explicit, and these plans are often sold under an advertising rhetoric that distorts the situation.

In individual instances, such as in Medi-Cal in California, clear deception and falsification were evident in some HMO marketing efforts, but to dwell on these abuses misses the larger point. Even in the reputable plans, the scope of promised services is more than the plan was meant to provide, and a variety of barriers are put in the way of the consumer who attempts to obtain them. For example, enrollees are told that HMOs are organized to provide care as early as possible in sickness episodes. What they are not told is that HMOs eliminate economic barriers to access but replace these with a variety of bureaucratic impediments and limitations on the resources provided that keep enrollees from using too many services (Mechanic 1976a). While HMOs may still be the "best deals in town"—and I am inclined to believe that they are—they are sometimes marketed in a way that is misleading to the consumer. Similarly, many of the nonprofit and profit insurance plans are so complex and described in such esoteric terms that even an expert consumer cannot do serious comparison shopping.

Conflicts in Values, Expectations, and Incentives

In the research process, conflicts are apparent between research goals and optimal adherence to patients' rights. The research investigator naturally wishes to carry out his studies in the most effective way and in a fashion that utilizes his efforts and resources most economically. The consideration of patients' rights may require that he modify his design from scientifically optimal procedures or invest greater time in certain phases of the study to ensure that ethical requirements are met. In short, these two sets of values must be balanced in some way. Violations of patients' rights often stem from the emphasis given to research values and from the investigator's wish to enhance his reputation or professional career. In the arena of service delivery, in contrast, conflicts are more likely to arise from the economic context and economic incentives implicit in the ways services are organized and professionals are paid. The pattern and mix of services provided tend to be shaped substantially by the mode of remuneration; the prevalence of services performed reflects whether services are paid for directly and at what level of remuneration (Glaser 1970).

In the fee-for-service sector it is usually in the physician's interest to carry out numerous technical procedures, because doing so is remunerative. Such a fee structure creates incentives for the performance of discretionary services, and it is maintained that much excess surgery, overutilization of hospitals, and unnecessary diagnostic and laboratory procedures are a result of such economic incentives (see, for example, Fuchs 1974). These tendencies toward excessive treatment (Fuchs 1968) are facilitated by the uncertainty of much of medical practice and the lack of clear norms as to the

Conclusion

The ethical problems in service delivery are both varied and complex, and there are real dangers in an approach that tries to respond to each new problem as it becomes apparent by writing new guidelines and rules. Such regulation in the aggregate not only involves high administrative cost but also feeds skepticism and contempt from those whose behavior the rules are intended to influence. More modest efforts, better fitted to the realities of organizational behavior, may induce a more sensitive response to the interests and needs of patients. Two major principles emerge from this discussion.

First, inequalities in power between patients and providers are greatest and most troublesome when the patient lacks a choice. This argues very strongly for maximizing "dual choice" in the insurance and health delivery marketplace. In any case, problems will continue when choices cannot be readily provided, as in many government programs for the poor and also in the private sector when geography or the complexity of the care required argues for only one source of service. Second, when problems arise, clear mechanisms should exist to help clarify and rectify them. Educational mechanisms are preferable to more aversive ones.

There is growing indication that patient rights are of increasing concern to the Congress and to the Executive Branch. Should further intervention efforts be undertaken, it would be desirable to avoid response to each salient problem by specific rule formulation. A more constructive approach would encourage programs to develop adequate grievance mechanisms, ombudsmen, and other devices that facilitate communication and feedback relevant to troublesome problems. While medical care involves real conflicts of interest, there are many areas where good will, effective feedback, and mutual respect would enhance the quality of services far more than any attempt to govern behavior by the proliferation of rules.

V | Health Services and Behavioral Research

10 | Monitoring the Health-Care System: Health-Services Research

The health-care industry is an extraordinarily large and complex arena and has undergone enormous growth and diversification in the past decade. Research organized to monitor its performance, to identify impending problems, and to formulate alternative approaches constitutes a small but important effort for the future. The field of health-services research focuses on the production, organization, distribution, and impact of health services on health status, illness, and disability. Although it shares certain concerns with behavioral studies, such as the determinants of health status, reactions to illness, health-promotive behavior, and factors affecting adherence to medical advice, it concentrates attention on the ways in which the distribution, quality, effectiveness, and efficiency of the medical-care process can be improved. Because health-services research also is often associated with demonstration projects and problems of technology transfer, these relationships require consideration despite the different emphases in demonstration and research programs.

Charles Lewis (1977) has raised serious questions about the links between health-services research and policy formulation and implementation. In a response to Lewis' review of the low visibility of health-services research and its uncertain impact, J. M. Last (1977) reports that a similar study he carried out, but did not publish, found comparable results. It might be anticipated that health-services research would be an area of vigorous and accelerating research activity given its pragmatic focus on such issues of national concern as cost containment, access to care, and assurance of quality. Instead, the field faces considerable skepticism among public officials and an erosion of its research and training support (National Research Coun-

cil 1977). Lewis' article illustrates the extent to which leaders in the
health field are confused about the content and functions of such
research activity. Clarification of criteria for evaluating the role and
performance of health-services research is required for an appropriate
judgment.

Vulnerability of the Health-Services Research Sector

The health-services research field is relatively young (U.S. President's Science Advisory Committee Panel 1972)—having received
major research support only in the last two decades—and thus is
extremely vulnerable to instability in financing and uninformed
criticism. Most scientific activity is organized around disciplines with
distinctive perspectives and professional organizations that serve as a
basis for identification and effective lobbying. Health-services research, in contrast, is carried out by members of a variety of
disciplines, such as physicians, sociologists, epidemiologists, biostatis-
ticians, economists, or operations researchers. Although shared research concerns bring these professionals together, they have no clear
organizational affiliation or professional identification around the
health-services research area. Most such research workers identify
with their primary discipline, making it difficult to measure the
research manpower available or even the boundaries of the field
(National Research Council 1977). Moreover, unlike the various
interest groups representing the study of such diseases as cancer,
heart disease, and mental illness, or highly organized disciplinary
groups such as biochemists or psychologists who maintain staff to
promote their disciplinary involvements, health-services research has
no organized constituency to promote it. Because health-services
research lacks the emotional appeal of categorical disease problems
or the professional organization of the traditional disciplines, support
for the field must rest solely on its merits and potential. In this
respect, the field continues to be handicapped by unrealistic expectations, inflated demands, and erratic modifications of its research
agendas by funding agencies.

Although most basic research fields are oriented toward a particular community of scholars who share many assumptions, perspectives, and methodological styles, health-services research speaks more
directly to policymakers and administrators who are typically faced

with pressing practical problems. Health-services research must not only achieve a level of scientific rigor satisfactory to the professional community, who scrutinize its theories and research efforts, but must also pose issues in a way that appears reasonable to those faced with decisions. The expectations of scientific rigor of one's colleagues often interfere with meeting the expectations of simplicity, comprehensibility, and lack of qualification demanded by the policymaker. One never hears administrators or legislators complaining that research in immunology is worthless because they cannot understand it, but we frequently are told that health-services research funding is being wasted on "incomprehensible regression equations." Thus, health-services research faces not only the usual needs of a research discipline but also the additional expectation of suitable translation.

The Role of Health-Services Research

Health-services research constitutes a minuscule effort relative to the magnitude of the industry it scrutinizes, the intellectual scope of the problems it deals with, and the social and political context in which it must operate. Such research commonly deals with problems that involve strong ideologies, competing perspectives, and contending interests. Often the solutions desired are not simply technical and scientific but also decisions about values, and yet the researcher is frequently admonished for his timidity in suggesting clearly and without equivocation what should be done. Although administrators are not so naive to anticipate that health-services research could resolve political disputes, such research can conveniently serve as a scapegoat for those who feel frustrated by the difficulties of modifying the health-care arena in any fundamental way.

The most serious problem affecting the future of health-services research efforts is the expectation that a modest research investment will provide solutions to the political dilemmas of health care. It is both naive and counterproductive to anticipate any direct relationship between such research and policy implementation. The demand that health-services research questions be formulated in terms of immediate political issues, moreover, debases the processes of problem formulation, compromises adequate data acquisition, and inevitably leads to disappointment and frustration. To the extent that policy decisions are important, highly visible, and affect important stakes for contending interests, their shape will depend more on political compromise than on results of particular research projects, although research results may help indirectly to inform the debate and shape the outcome. Although legislators may ask what research project ever led to a specific policy decision, the implication being that such research is of little value and unworthy of support, the fact is that the question is itself based on false and unrealistic premises. Health-services research will (and, indeed, should) always be in the background in the formulation of important policy decisions unless the decisions are purely technical ones. And few important health-services issues are simply matters of knowledge or technical expertise.

Health-services research cannot solve the big policy issues, but it performs a wide variety of functions, including acquisition of descriptive information on the performance of the health services, analytic research and hypothesis testing on microissues—such as the effects of cost sharing on consumers or variations in remuneration on professionals—and evaluation of large sociomedical programs. It also is allied closely with demonstration programs in which the emphasis is less on theory and more on the practical issues of implementation and the diffusion of innovations. The major role of health-services research is to inform the climate of policymaking and implementation and not to determine the decisions or actions initiated, although there are occasional exceptions on matters that are largely technical and relatively apolitical. Through a variety of types of health-services research, issues are raised, observations are made, and perspectives are developed that over the long term affect the way administrators and politicians see the problems, formulate options and approaches, and implement decisions. To the extent that such research does this job well, it contributes immensely to intelligent policy consideration and more than repays the relatively small investment involved. Unless we take a fairly long-range perspective, we may readily miss the extent to which our conceptions of health-care problems have changed in the past decade or two, in large part because of such research.

Although two decades ago most observers had an implicit faith that greater investments in providing health services would significantly improve the health of the nation, there now is much greater skepticism that large marginal increases in health-care investments bring commensurate results (Knowles 1977b). We are now much more aware that the health status of the nation depends on environmental nunerating physicians by capitation or salary in contrast to fee-for-vice, and on the performance of nurse practitioners as compared h physicians. Such studies are very diverse in their concerns and y reflect the state of current knowledge, the ingenuity of the estigator, the variations present in the health-care system, the sibilities of initiating new programs and experiments, and the its of research personnel and funding. Although in the long run ny of these studies will not be particularly useful to the policy-ker, they make up the intellectual resources of the health-services d and serve as the basis for new ideas. Thus such investments must seen in a probabilistic sense; it is essential to fund a broad range of dies to generate those that will importantly affect thinking and re efforts. As with biomedical research, it is necessary to explore ly paths with the knowledge that some will be cul-de-sacs.

Although administrators can define certain areas of present inter-there is no effective way of targeting such knowledge-building rts. A modest but stable research program is needed to facilitate work of academic researchers who generate ideas based on their theories, observations, and experience. Certainly a field as large health services can afford this risk capital, which ensures that at t some segment of research goes beyond the current notions of relevant and the practical.

uation Research

Another type of effort involves evaluation of new and ongoing grams. Such studies are particularly difficult and frequently dis-ointing, because the goals of many programs are not clearly ned or agreed upon. Often the coalition necessary to put a ram together involves groups with varying goals and definitions, maintaining a vague symbolic definition of the program's pur-serves important political needs. No one may really expect the ram to have the impact suggested by political rhetoric, and it be pointless to study whether it really does. Other barriers to lation include the reluctance of administrators to put themselves sk of a negative assessment, the tendency to modify programs atedly before an evaluation is completed, thus complicating and rmining the evaluation, and a variety of methodological prob-inherent in any complex evaluative effort.

conditions and patterns of behavior outside the health-care delivery system. We increasingly realize that the resources available—such as hospital beds, surgical specialists, and primary-care physicians—affect the magnitude of demand and utilization and that there is an uncertain relationship between the use of more services and health status (Fuchs 1974). We have learned to see problems of providing physician and other services not simply as issues of numbers but also as problems of distribution, and we are targeting our policies more specifically on the basis of such knowledge (Lewis, Fein, and Mechanic 1976). We have learned a great deal about the benefits and problems of health-maintenance organizations and the ways they compare with alternative delivery systems. The value and limitations of introducing a wide variety of new personnel and facilities—such as physician assistants, nurse practitioners, perinatal units, and surgi-centers—are now widely appreciated. We have better knowledge of the imperfections of the medical marketplace and more understanding of the ways to deal with them than before, and we have acquired more knowledge of the relationship between modes of financing and professional remuneration and the manner in which services are produced. Although all of this may resemble the conventional wisdom of the day, the fact is that it was not the conventional wisdom of yesterday, and much of the way we see things has been informed by the results of health-services research.

Unlike research in most other disciplines, successful health-services research attracts critics. Although we all applaud new developments in cancer research, in the understanding of schizophrenia, or in the improvement of care for the patient with kidney disease, research on the performance of the health sector is frequently politically costly to particular professional groups. Surgeons hardly like the suggestion that they perform unnecessary surgery; hospitals dislike the implication that they are inefficient and wasteful; and physicians recoil at suggestions that they create their own demand, that their care is ineffective or of poor quality, and that they maintain political control over the medical marketplace. One hardly expects these groups to serve as a constituency in support of their critics.

The fact is, however, that a well-structured health-services research program is essential to future health-care policy and to adequate monitoring of a massive national investment. Almost every recent major piece of health legislation poses requirements for data acquisition, planning, and evaluation for which we lack the resources and often the theoretical and methodological sophistication as well.

Problems and questions posed quite glibly in political debate are often difficult to translate into scientific hypotheses that can be examined in any reasonable fashion. Although it is natural for those who want immediate answers to be impatient, many of the questions raised are complex and difficult to study and require long-term conceptual and empirical efforts. These considerations should make clear that health-services research is much more likely to contribute successfully if its concerns are more long-term than short-range and if its efforts can be separated from the pressing needs of policymakers and administrators, who may require the guidance of informed persons but who are unlikely to benefit in any immediate sense from research. With these considerations in mind, we will consider the functions of the health-services research sector in more detail below.

Information and Intelligence

One of the most acute needs of those with administrative responsibilities is simply to know the facts: facts concerning the gaps in the distribution of services, the actual costs for medical and surgical procedures in varying localities, the relationship between expenditures and changes in health status, the rates of admission to hospitals and lengths of stay for varying procedures and the ways they are changing, the costs of new technologies and how they affect physician behavior and medical outcomes, and many more. Moreover, administrators require some indication of impending problems both to formulate responses and to deal with possible political contingencies. Although we know a great deal about the performance of the health services, there are many crucial facts we still lack despite their importance for future planning. Many such efforts to gather important facts routinely or on a periodic basis are made through the National Center for Health Statistics and a variety of special surveys carried out by health-survey researchers in universities, such as those on access to care and expenditures for care carried out through the Center for Health Administration Studies at the University of Chicago.

Acquiring facts is not simple, because they depend on concepts that may be unclear or difficult to measure. What is the meaning of a physician visit when the content of such visits varies widely from one context to another and includes office visits and phone visits? How

does one estimate the prevalence of psychiatric dis[...] perts disagree on appropriate case definitions? How [...] sure the impact of medical care on health status wh[...] and reliable measures of the dependent variable? How [...] the total expenditures for physician services when [...] expenditures are aggregated with hospital charges[...] simple facts are serious conceptual problems and [...] issues that continue to require considerable develop[...] we are to generate reliable information for sound dec[...]

In addition to routine monitoring through large-[...] statistical reporting systems, there is need for more [...] information on how the epidemiology of disease is [...] community, the types of case mix seen in varying t[...] the procedures and costs generated by varying t[...] encounters, and the impact of changing patterns [...] work, new technologies, and innovative facilities. W[...] are the case-fatality rates for varying types of med[...] procedures in varying types of facilities? Are ph[...] doing more laboratory procedures in routine medic[...] how does the amount of such work vary by t[...] organizational setting, or type of patient? What is th[...] released from institutions as part of the emphasis [...] ization programs? What services are they receivin[...] are they having, and what is their level of funct[...] types of community settings? Although it is diff[...] which of the many descriptive questions concerni[...] will become special agenda items for policy m[...] descriptive efforts both contribute to the anticipa[...] problems and provide a data base from which to [...] political options.

Analytic Research and Hypothesis Testing

Health-services research also includes more co[...] may not have immediate relevance but contribute [...] informing policy. Such studies generally involve [...] about the impacts of various types of incentives [...] tions. Such studies might include hypotheses a[...] coinsurance and deductibles on rates of utilizatio[...]

the culture of institutions. It constitutes perhaps the most difficult and problematic area in the entire health-services arena.

The transfer of health-services organizational arrangements, as in the development of HMOs, has many of the same problems as the transfer of biomedical knowledge and technology, but it is infinitely more complex in a political and sociological sense. In the case of the transfer of biomedical technologies, such as new drugs or computed tomographic scanning (a noninvasive technique producing cross-sectional images of the head and body), there may be no major organizational changes required, and the adoption of the innovation may be consistent with existing ideological and economic interests. There still remains the problem, however, of teaching large dispersed populations of physicians to use the technology wisely and when indicated. Although new technologies may be adopted quickly, they may be used inappropriately, as is evident in relatively simple cases such as the prescription of antibiotics. However, when organizational innovations are at issue, they more commonly require fundamental modifications in professional alignments and routines, and they may threaten the roles, statuses, and economic security of particular individuals or groups. Thus it is much easier for a group of physicians to accept a new drug or a new diagnostic practice than to introduce a nurse practitioner into their practice or change in any fundamental way how they relate to patients. The fact that Kaiser can organize HMOs that perform reasonably well, thus, is no assurance that other organizations lacking similar histories, ideological commitments, leadership, and experience can achieve the same outcomes.

The problems associated with transfer of innovations define a large agenda of needed health-services research. Because conditions vary from one setting to another, it is essential to replicate and monitor innovations in a variety of settings to identify the extent to which they differ in performance. Such replications are also necessary to reassure new adopters that the success of the innovation was not dependent solely on the special skills of those who initiated it, but that the idea is adaptable to settings like their own. Repeated studies of nurse-practitioner deployment, for example, build a momentum that breaks down barriers to the use of such personnel among physicians, who come to feel more secure in trying new approaches once they see others successfully doing so.

We need improved understanding of how to support innovations that tend to be fragile and easily undermined. The bind of traditional practice is very strong, and most organizational innovations either fail or take on more conventional coloration. Also, we need a better grasp of the factors that explain why some innovations diffuse rapidly while others that are successfully executed are never repeated. Although stable funding that allows an innovation to develop is a crucial factor, we need a more precise delineation of the incentives, cultural conditions, and technical support required to encourage more rapid deployment of useful innovations.

Conclusion

Administrators and policymakers are frequently impatient with health-services research that is not immediately relevant and practical. They question the value of research that does not directly result in policy implementation and that deals with more abstract theoretical and methodological issues. Health-services research, however, has affected the climate of policymaking and the options considered to a much larger degree than is generally recognized and has achieved this more through long-range efforts and basic studies than through an emphasis on immediate practicality.

The fact is that the same basic issues and dilemmas in health care have persisted for years, suggesting that the problem is not the failure to focus on the practical but rather the economic, political, and ideological barriers that make it so difficult to reach an effective consensus. Although at any given point in time the administrator's options are limited, understanding problems in the long term sharpens policy thinking and contributes to successful policy formulation. Fundamental examination of questions dealing with cost containment, professional behavior, forces affecting health, and consumer attitudes and response within a broad context will suggest perspectives and options likely to inform the climate of future action. The health industry is enormous in size and complex in organization and increasingly faces difficult social, economic, and ethical dilemmas. Health-services research is a small but valuable endeavor that provides basic understanding of the way the health sector functions and its impact on the population. Maintaining and further developing such research activity are investments worthy of our attention and support.

11 | Behavioral Research and Health: The Need for a Broad View

Patterns of health and illness are deeply embedded in the socio-cultural environment, in the manner in which people think and behave, and in the currents of social change that affect their lives. As medical science has successfully contained the morbidity and mortality associated with infectious disease, the core of medical care has shifted to chronic and degenerative diseases and those substantially affected by patterns of behavior and social organization. The change in disease patterns and associated demands for medical care have been sufficiently dramatic so that there is common reference to the "new morbidity" (Haggerty, Roghmann, and Pless 1975), with implications that medical care must become more responsive to these emerging patterns. For example, the change in typical problems dealt with by the pediatrician, with a growing emphasis on developmental and behavioral concerns, requires very different knowledge and skills from those traditionally taught.

At the level of ambulatory medical care, it is evident that much of the demand arises from psychosocial factors relating to the occurrence of discomfort and disability, to the need for support or secondary gain because of difficulties in the family or at work, or to inappropriately learned patterns of illness behavior. Behavioral patterns such as smoking, excessive drinking, promiscuous use of drugs, poor nutrition, little exercise, high risk taking, and violence contribute to much of the evident disease, injury, and disability. The major types of illness causing death or serious disability—such as heart disease, cancer, stroke, and mental disorders—are at best amenable only to ameliorative efforts, ones that are enormously expensive for the uncertain results achieved through the use of halfway tech-

137

nologies. In areas having preventive possibilities—such as hypertension control, smoking behavior, and diet—the problems are substantially behavioral and not well developed within the context of current medical approaches.

We have yet to achieve integration of effective behavioral strategies into the everyday provision of medical care. In part, this reflects the force of traditional assumptions and practice in the provision of care; in part, it reflects the small component in behavioral training in the training of the young physician; but perhaps most important, it reflects the fragmentation and uncertainty of much of our behavioral knowledge and the difficulty of successfully adapting that knowledge to the care of patients within the current mode of approach. Although behavioral science offers some exciting leads for medical care, there is need for much greater development of such knowledge as well as serious reconsideration of the appropriate context for applying what we have learned.

There is a tendency to think of behavioral strategies simply as the application of one-to-one care, as in curative medicine. Although there will be obvious applications at the individual treatment level for those who already suffer from disabilities resulting from behavior or social patterns more generally, greater potentialities may exist in applying the knowledge we acquire in relation to larger groups or communities using the work place, the family, the school, and other centers of social interaction as the foci for preventive efforts. While such efforts must face the realities of existing social mores and values, and political and economic barriers, examining the issues in a broad way may suggest some promising possibilities for research and intervention other than those characterized by traditional medical-care approaches.

Technology versus Education: A Persistent Dilemma

Although decisions about whether it is more productive to pursue basic causes as compared with developing ameliorative technologies depend on the state of knowledge and scientific opportunities in any particular area, they also involve value judgments. Our thinking about social behavior implies certain philosophical commitments, such as the issue of personal responsibility. In the area of health education, for example, strong free-will ideologies prevail, and there are frequent suggestions that persons who injure themselves through their own behavior are blameworthy. Yet it is abundantly clear that the techniques we have to shape or alter behavior, even among highly motivated persons, are often ineffective. Moreover, healthful behavior may seriously conflict with other valued goals and commitments.

In some areas, as in the accident field, large efforts in driver education, safety appeals, and mass-media promotion have had relatively modest influence on driving patterns, the use of seat restraints, or alcohol-related driving. An increasing number of persons involved in the accident field are convinced that the most effective community strategy to preserve health is to develop technological protections in contrast to educational or behavioral-change efforts. More progress, they argue, will come from improved vehicles, better roads, and protective technologies such as air bags in automobiles. Studies show that drivers do not use seat restraints despite awareness of their effectiveness (Robertson 1976). While some might argue that the community need not assume responsibility and incur additional costs for those who are imprudent, the fact that the technological approach will significantly save lives and prevent injuries is quite compelling.

There are examples in which the "technological fix" presents a more uncertain alternative. Consider the common instance in medical care in which patients suffer distress because of problems in their lives and social circumstances. These problems are then reflected in a variety of physical complaints such as anxiety, fatigue, headaches, and insomnia. Many of these patients are given drugs to alleviate their symptoms, and psychoactive drugs have become the most commonly prescribed medications in primary care. Patients often abuse these drugs, and some become drug dependent. Although such therapy is an expedient and expeditious approach, considering the many such patients that busy doctors must deal with, the value of such symptomatic treatment as a substitute for greater self-awareness and improved coping skills is open to question. Symptomatic treatment is often necessary and useful, but it rarely solves the troubling issues. Time and patience are required in assisting such patients to define more appropriately what their troubles really are and what might be done about them. Some troubles are not remediable, but symptomatic treatment by itself may help induce chronic patienthood. The fact is that the necessary assistance many patients need does not require a physician or even a health professional. What may be needed are better self-help and community structures that provide the required support and coping opportunities. Indeed, many of the problems patients bring to doctors may be an outgrowth of the fragmentation of community itself.

Community, Disease, and Medical Care

There is a long tradition in sociological studies examining human malaise and maladaptive behavior from the perspective of social integration. Since Durkheim's (1951) classic investigations of social integration and suicide, there has been continuing interest in the ways in which loss of status or meaning and breakdown in social cohesion contribute to psychological and physical distress. Such events, defined in various ways, have been found to be associated with physical and psychological disorder and early death. Consider, for example, the accumulating evidence that marital dissolution is associated with high mortality and excesses of a variety of diseases (Lynch 1977), or the impressive evidence that unemployment and decreases in per capita income are associated with increases in a wide spectrum of disease mortality (Brenner 1976). Surely some of these findings reflect social selection processes, but they are not fully accounted for by such factors. Health and disease are related to processes of hope, meaning, and identity, and when these are impaired they take their toll biologically as well as socially. While intriguing, however, such observations are not very helpful in isolating the specific life processes that must be understood to allow us to intervene effectively. Incomplete knowledge, of course, can be valuable. John Snow understood little about the specific causes of cholera or the dynamics of the disease, but the recording of the pattern of occurrence of the disease identified the sources of infection and allowed them to be controlled. Similarly, although we may lack precise understanding of the dynamic relationship between employment and health, it would be prudent to work on the assumption of a causal relationship while we seek more knowledge because such an assumption is also consistent with other important goals.

Adaptation to new challenges or threats depends on the individual's preparation to deal with them successfully. Although we usually think of preparation at the individual level as the skills and psychological resources of the person that make coping possible, such preparation is most typically patterned by the sociocultural environment, by socialization, and by the natural incentives and supports that are characteristic of kinship groups, neighborhoods, and community. The breakdown of community, thus, involves the dropping away of the routine and expected resources that are necessary to deal with uncertain or even typical events. It also may involve the dissolution of meaning, identity, belongingness, and incentive, because it is the idea of community that gives action a sense of relevance.

Meaning is more difficult to sustain as technology and communication bombard individuals with alternatives that make all events and norms seem relative. Social change is disruptive because it not only challenges explanations for the cause of things but also plays havoc with traditional and typical social alignments. As populations face change as a matter of course, they develop social institutions and skills that allow better adaptation to its disruptions, and the design of social structure may provide more or less opportunity for effective adaptation to change. Many persons have difficulty in defining meaningful and comfortable alignments, and problems of adaptation result. When the social structure does not provide resources to cope with disruptive changes or other adversities, people seek palliatives. These palliatives may include alcohol, drugs, risk taking, or dependence on the medical-care system. Although it is quite typical for cohesive subcultures to develop within more heterogeneous environments and for these subcultures to serve as a basis for social integration and identity, a highly mobile and changing sociocultural environment makes such attachments more tenuous and more open to threat.

The lack of social integration is only one of many sources of stress, but social support is important in any case as a buffer against other types of challenges to material well-being, identity, and self-esteem. Social support provides not only a sense of belonging but also a variety of tangible assets such as the sharing of resources, assistance, and time. It also involves communication that the person is valued, cared for, and esteemed (Cobb 1976). Although the former may be easily measured, the latter is a subtle communication process that involves empathy with the position of the person under stress. It may require constructive criticism as well as approval, nonintrusiveness as well as an involvement in the other's affairs. In short, providing support is not easily defined or taught.

In the literature on stress and disease, two conceptions have remained prominent. The first views stress as arising from the individual's negative appraisal of his situation, while the second defines stress as life change that requires modifications of the individual's efforts and life routines (Mechanic 1978a:222-46). While the appraisal view concentrates on events perceived as stressful by the persons involved, such as those involving loss of love, status, or valued possessions, the life-change view is based on the notion that change itself, however it is appraised, contributes to the occurrence of disease. Both conceptions may be correct, depending on the disease condition under consideration. Although depression may result primarily in situations in which individuals experience losses they feel helpless to affect, life change itself if sufficiently protracted over time may contribute to the occurrence of such conditions as cardiovascular disease irrespective of the person's affect. Cardiovascular processes have been conditioned by a long evolutionary history, and in the short run may not adapt well to major shifts in living conditions.

A major task of behavioral investigation in medicine is to define and classify patients using medical-care services more precisely and to study alternative modes of assistance for those whose basic problem is anxiety, depression, or demoralization. Such alternatives as self-help groups, relaxation therapy, counseling, psychoactive drug treatment, and general supportive care need to be evaluated relative to varying types of problems within this population. Means of involving these disaffected persons in social enterprises to provide new meanings and identities need to be explored. Above all, we require a more detailed understanding of the development of patterns of psychological morbidity, the precise processes involved, and the ways in which they may be short-circuited before they become patterned as part of a chronic syndrome.

Implications of Behavioral Research

In recent years there have been many exciting leads linking behavioral processes to body responses. Exciting potentials exist in such fields as biofeedback, operant processes, and attribution approaches. We are increasingly learning more about the role of stress and coping, the functions of supportive structures, and processes of social influence. The gaps in our knowledge are still very large, however, and there are many uncertainties in translating laboratory and field results for practical application. Consider, for example, the growing field of research linking the so-called Type A personality and coronary heart disease. The Type A behavior pattern is associated with hard-driving and achievement-oriented behavior, time urgency, and hostility. The results linking this behavior pattern with risk of disease and mortality have been intriguing but continue to leave many questions unanswered. Friedman and Rosenman have encouraged a national intervention effort to attempt to change this behavior pattern, but without any evidence that such change can be achieved or produce the desired outcomes (Friedman and Rosenman 1974).

Although studies of Type A seem to reveal something very important about behavioral traits implicated in coronary heart disease, the conception of the nature of the type, its most important components, and its relationship to biological processes remain vague. Jenkins (1976) maintains that this behavior pattern is not a stressful situation or a disturbed response, and Friedman and Rosenman argue that it is "not a complex of worries or fears or phobias or obsessions," but it remains unclear exactly what it is. While Jenkins speaks of "a style of behavior with which some persons habitually respond to circumstances that arouse them" and "a deeply ingrained, enduring trait," these notations fail to depict a clear concept of personality or of social development that accounts for the behaviors involved or their relation to biological processes.

What has been said of Type A behavior may be said of many other areas in behavioral investigation. In a number of areas there have been exciting leads that have tremendous potential for improving health status and the provision of medical care. What is needed is not immediate implementation, although such information should be used when appropriate, but more detailed investigation and demonstration that refines our knowledge and specifies the phenomena in question more clearly. The number of suggestions of potential therapeutic significance is considerable, but they have to be pursued in a systematic and rigorous fashion. To cite a few examples: What is the explanation for the almost universally observed excess in depression among women as compared with men (Weissman and Klerman 1977)? Is clinical depression related to a pattern of learned helplessness (Seligman 1975), and can such patterns be unlearned? What are the specific types of instruction and types of communication that minimize distress during medical procedures and that maximize the degree of adherence to medical advice (Leventhal 1970) in such crucial areas as hypertension and diabetes control? What factors account for such voluntary giving of help as donation of blood (Titmuss 1971), and through what techniques can such giving be enhanced? How can biofeedback techniques be used to facilitate self-regulation of noxious physiological states (Miller 1975), and what long-term impact can it have on the occurrence of illness and disability? What types of psychological and social management best contain disability associated with the occurrence of chronic disease (Mechanic 1977b), and how can social support and guided attributional processes prevent secondary disabilities often associated with physical illness and defects? Why do antisocial children have such a poor prognosis and a wide range of disorders in adult life (Robins 1966), and what types of psychological and social interventions might best moderate these destructive processes? Researchers in behavior and health are presently pursuing many questions of theoretical and practical importance for improving health, but in almost every case our knowledge is incomplete and uncertain, and more basic and long-term investigation is required.

The fact is that social policies of enormous consequence for the nation have been initiated on incomplete and often defective data. In the area of the treatment of the mentally ill, for example, a vast shift from mental hospitals to community care has occurred in the past two decades, as described in chapter 6, with increasing numbers of patients living in single-room dwellings, board and care facilities, nursing homes, and a variety of transitional settings. Although this shift was facilitated by the introduction of psychotropic drugs in the 1950s, much of the impetus came from changing administrative perspectives, new ideologies, and financial pressures. There have been many positive features of deinstitutionalization, but it is often associated with new social costs, low levels of functioning among many patients in these facilities, and a variety of new problems of social control. Knowledge of the best ways to organize services in the community for impaired patients, or understanding the community contexts and programs that best facilitated their adjustment in the community and enhanced the quality of their lives, has been meager at best (Segal and Aviram 1978). Many of the problems associated with deinstitutionalization are just beginning to be examined in a systematic way. What is the long-term performance of different types of patients on psychoactive drugs? What degree of social stimulation and social support is necessary to ensure maintenance of living skills and competence without triggering new psychotic episodes? What techniques allow families to cope with the disturbed behavior of schizophrenic members without undue damage to the unit or the social development of children? At this point we have only the most fragmentary knowledge of the way community living environments affect the problems and levels of functioning associated with community care.

There are numerous areas in which we desperately need improved behavioral knowledge for sound implementation of social policy. Although it is dangerous to expect too much too soon from the behavioral sciences in solving difficult social problems, it is prudent to maintain and develop the capacity to pursue promising leads in a systematic and rigorous way. As someone involved closely with medicine in the past twenty years, I have always been impressed with the double standard that prevails in building behavioral-science capacities as compared with those in the biological and physical sciences. While no medical school dean would hire one or two physiologists or biochemists and direct them to solve the problems of human physiology, behavioral scientists are constantly asked to solve impossible problems rather than being accepted as scientists building another area of knowledge slowly and meticulously. When behavioral scientists allow unrealistic expectations to prevail rather than defining carefully what they can in fact do, disillusionment is likely. The behavioral sciences must be seen as one more group of sciences relevant to medicine that require similar types of research support, rather than as a source of prophecies with quick fixes for difficult social problems. The next chapter describes one area—health and illness behavior—illustrating the complexity of concepts and research approaches necessary to achieve the understanding essential to effective application.

12

Behavioral Research and Health: The Study of Health and Illness Behavior

In the previous chapter it was argued that behavioral scientists must be allowed to pursue the development of their knowledge base if they are to achieve the understanding necessary to deal effectively with problems of importance. In this chapter I will illustrate some approaches to studying an area of vital importance to the operation of our medical-care system—the manner in which patients perceive illness and use medical care. I noted in chapter 2 that one mode of reducing demand for services is to modify the ways people respond to their health and symptoms and relate to the medical-care system. Although in theory this constitutes an important policy option, in reality we know too little about such patterns, the functions they serve, or the ways to change them to justify major policy interventions at this level. I will show that the problems of illness behavior are more complex than they may seem and that there is much we have yet to learn.

In modern society there has been increasing medicalization of social problems and a growing reliance on physicians to deal with a wide variety of complaints and difficulties. Problems that were formerly dealt with by family, neighborhood, and church are now commonly managed within the health-care arena. Some see this as an alarming trend that detracts from the responsibility of persons to care for themselves and that so floods the medical-care system that too little time is available for those who are "seriously ill." What is needed, they argue, is a reduction of community dependence on the medical-care structure and the development of community alternatives that allow human problems to be managed without medical intervention.

146

There are no clear criteria to specify when the medical system is being overutilized. From one perspective, overutilization can be defined as instances when persons seek care for conditions but physicians have little ability to intervene effectively. If this criterion, however, should be adopted, then much of medical care fits it, and it applies to extraordinarily serious and incapacitating illnesses as well as minor ones. The definition can be refined by applying it only to instances of illness that are not life-threatening and not incapacitating. But the definition of incapacitating is itself arbitrary, and physicians and patients often have different views of the matter. Although psychological distress, insomnia, and fatigue may seem trivial to some physicians, many patients who have such problems suffer a great deal and seek palliative care. An examination of physicians' definitions of trivial illness suggests that they tend to categorize as trivial problems those that seem vague and that they feel they can do little about or problems that are known to be self-limited and that benefit little from medical intervention. Although the former perception reflects the stance of medicine and the insecurities of the physician, the latter speaks more to the patterns of patients' illness behavior.

Many discussions view the use of medical services as a market process subject to price variations and the pattern of supply, but economic factors offer only a partial explanation of utilization behavior. Although economists disagree on the degree of elasticity of medical care, there is consensus that it is modest, even in instances in which consumers control the purchasing decision, as in the case of drugs or ambulatory physician visits. The problems of overutilization may be exacerbated when the service is substantially insured so patients do not have to calculate the true cost of consumption and when supply is abundant, but utilization is also a complex behavioral problem reflecting sociocultural background and social development, situational difficulties, and personal and social integration. Thus the analysis of illness behavior and preventive health patterns serves as a model of health behavior more generally, elucidating the psychological complexities, the irrationalities, and the socially ingrained patterns that make change so difficult.

Concepts of Health and Disease

There is considerable evidence in both animals and human beings that altered psychological states—as induced by "learned helplessness," lack of predictability, hopelessness, distorted feedback, loss, and a variety of other stressors—affect bodily processes and the occurrence of disease (Dohrenwend and Dohrenwend 1974; Seligman 1975). Moreover, such factors condition the ways people define health and illness, respond to symptoms and incapacity, and utilize the medical-care system (Mechanic 1978a). However much physicians may wish to reserve the process of medical care for those entities they conceive of as illness, it is the patients' conceptions of health and disease and their experiences in the community that determine the way the medical-care system comes to be utilized.

Physicians and patients tend to view health status in fundamentally different ways. Physicians are trained to identify discrete illnesses to the extent possible and have no adequate measures of holistic functioning, vitality, or well-being. Patients, in contrast, tend to view health more globally and experientially. Although they may become concerned about specific symptoms, they tend to view their health in terms of an overall sense of well-being and the extent to which the symptoms they experience disrupt their ability to function or interfere in some significant fashion with their life activities. A variety of studies indicate that people's feeling states influence their sense of physical well-being (Apple 1960; Bauman 1961). Persons reporting poor physical health are frequently depressed, feel neglected, have low morale, suffer from alienation, and are less satisfied with life (Maddox 1962). Although the causal sequence goes both ways, there seems little doubt that overall life experiences affect one's general sense of well-being.

Tessler and Mechanic (1978) analyzed four diverse data sets (using multivariate controls) to examine the role of psychological distress on perceptions of physical health. In each case, distress was a significant factor related to the perceptions of physical health. Moreover, in a prospective study of utilization among enrollees of a prepaid group practice, Tessler, Mechanic, and Dimond (1976) found that the level of psychological distress was a significant factor predicting utilization levels while controlling a wide range of other variables, including health-status measures.

While the concept of illness usually refers to a limited scientific concept denoting a constellation of symptoms or a condition underlying them (Mechanic 1978a:95–99), the term illness behavior describes the way in which persons respond to abnormal bodily indications. Illness behavior thus involves the manner in which a person monitors his body, defines and interprets his symptoms, takes remedial actions, and utilizes the health-care system. People differentially perceive, evaluate, and respond to illness, and such behaviors have enormous influence on the extent of the interference of illness with usual life routines, the chronicity of the condition, the obtaining of appropriate care, and the cooperation of the patient in the treatment situation.

The concept of preventive health behavior, in contrast, refers to patterns of response relating to health when the person has no specific symptoms. Traditionally, it has been used to study people's orientations toward preventive-care services such as immunizations, medical checkups, hypertension screening, and prophylactic dentistry (Becker 1974). Work in this area has been dominated by the health-belief model, which examines the extent to which a person sees a problem as having serious consequences and a high probability of occurrence (Rosenstock 1960). The model is basically a psychological cost- benefit analysis in which action follows motives that are most salient and perceived as most valuable when the person has conflicting motives. The model also gives attention to cues to action, because investigations show that activating stimuli are necessary to bring about the necessary actions among motivated persons. More recent research indicates that it is also helpful if persons have a clear plan for translating their motives into action (Leventhal 1970).

Modes of Studying Illness Behavior: Methodological Considerations

Although there is a large medical literature on the patient's hidden agenda in seeking medical care and on a variety of related issues, medical researchers have had difficulty in posing the relevant issues in a manner amenable to empirical research. There are at least four ways in which illness behavior can be studied: as a disposition of the person, as a result of an interaction between personal and environmental factors in a community, as a response to the health-care-services system, or as a decision-making process.

The dispositional approach assumes that persons have a fairly stable orientation to respond to illness in particular ways and seeks to identify differences in these response patterns. While some persons tend to be stoical in the face of illness, others are matter-of-fact or hypochondriacal. While some patients seek care readily for even minor symptoms, others are reluctant to seek care for even life-threatening illnesses. There is considerable variability in people's responses from one situation to another and over time, and we have insufficient data on the stability of health and illness behavior patterns over time to feel fully confident in the dispositional assumption. Thus it is simply a convenience for the purposes of acquiring more knowledge.

Reactions to pain or dispositions to use various kinds of medical services may be measured by verbal reports of what respondents would do in hypothetical situations or by their actual behavior—such as consulting a psychiatrist, joining a self-help group, or practicing transcendental meditation. The fact of having used one of these services may serve as a proxy for the disposition, and the investigator then tries to identify the factors associated with the response of interest.

Most dispositional studies are efforts to understand the development of the behavior pattern. For example, most studies of illness show that women report symptoms more frequently than men do and that they use physicians and psychiatrists more frequently as well (Lewis and Lewis 1977). A variety of interpretations have been posited to account for these findings, but none has adequately explained all the available data. Interpretations for the sex differences include real differences in the prevalence of disorder, characteristics of the measures used and judgments made that reflect sex biases, women's lower thresholds to perceive symptoms, women's greater willingness to acknowledge symptoms and seek care, women's greater knowledge and interest in health matters, and different role responsibilities between the sexes that affect the use of services. Although each of these interpretations is given from time to time, few studies successfully compare competing explanations (Mechanic 1976b).

Significant differences in responses to pain and illness between the sexes are already apparent by the fourth grade and increase with age (Mechanic 1964). Aggregate data on sex and use of medical care suggest that women have higher rates of utilization at all ages except during childhood, when the mother probably makes most of the decisions for both boys and girls. Lewis and his colleagues (1975), however, have shown that sex differences in using a school health service were apparent among young children in an experimental child-initiated help-seeking system. How these differences arise, how they are sustained, and how they might be modified have crucial relevance in understanding how to increase the public's responsibility for appropriate health behavior.

One of the most typical approaches to studying illness behavior is to carry out epidemiological surveys and identify those using or not using certain types of care or those who engage in particular health and illness practices. Other data from the surveys are then used to account for these differences. Such surveys typically examine socio-demographic factors, distress, life-change events, and attitudes toward medical care. Among factors commonly found to be associated with utilization of medical care are quality and severity of symptoms, levels of distress, sex, inclination to use medical facilities, skepticism of medical care, and faith in doctors.

A major problem with most epidemiological studies of help seeking is that they fail to differentiate the extent to which various independent predictors affect utilization through their influence on the occurrence of symptoms and the extent to which they have an independent effect on the help-seeking pattern (Mechanic 1976c). Moreover, in concentrating on studying only one source of assistance, such as general physician services or a psychiatric clinic, these studies cannot differentiate factors that predict help seeking in general as compared with those that predict the use of a specific type of service. Studies of use of multiple agencies by a specified population are extremely difficult to execute because of the complexity of the American health-care system and modes of payment. These studies usually require an enrolled population using a defined set of help-seeking agencies.

Gurin and associates (1960), in a national survey of definitions and reactions to personal problems, suggested that different types of factors influence various aspects of the help-seeking process, such as identification of the problem, the decision to seek care, and the type of practitioner consulted. Greenley and Mechanic (1976) studied the patterns of use of helping facilities for psychological-distress syndromes among a large student population. Among the types of sources of help studied were psychiatrists, counseling services, religious counselors, general physicians, and some other agencies on campus. There was considerable overlap in the problems brought to different sources of help, and most predictors of help seeking were specific to particular sources of assistance.

A third approach to studying illness behavior is to focus on the processes through which persons identify and evaluate symptoms, make interpretations of their causes and implications, and decide on the types of help to seek. Persons experiencing changes in their feeling states and physical functioning attempt to make sense of what is happening, and they tend to examine different intuitive hypotheses about the seriousness of their problems and the need for assistance. A major dimension of this process is the way people evaluate the causes of a problem and the extent to which they attribute the problem to external factors, internal difficulties, or moral and existential issues. An important function of health education is to shape such processes of evaluation and attribution so that they culminate in an effective pattern of care. Understanding attribution processes and the ways to modify them has many rehabilitative implications (Mechanic 1977b).

For example, during World War II soldiers who experienced "breakdowns" in combat were evacuated to the back lines, and their disorganized behavior was interpreted as a product of early childhood socialization. This provided the soldier with an excuse for maintaining his behavior and one that made it difficult to return him to a functioning role. The military later developed a policy that defined combat stress reactions as transient responses. Although soldiers were given opportunities to rest, the behavior was defined as a normal reaction to prolonged stress, and most soldiers were expected to return to active duty. As a result, there were many less psychiatric losses (Glass 1958). These policies are now used in community care of the mentally ill, and it is clear that patients suffering from considerable distress and impairment can continue to cope in many realms of their lives. Although such "normalization" can be carried too far, the evidence is that the encouragement of continued coping and activity often protects the patient from further deterioration and despair, and that patients are very much influenced by social expectations (Brown, Bone, Dalison, and Wing 1966).

The interpretation of symptoms may have a dramatic effect on the course of illness and disability. Many problems may be defined as inherent in a person or related to social, cultural, or environmental factors. An example is the growth of the women's movement, which has brought about a major shift in the way many women interpret the discomforts and dissatisfactions they feel. While prior to this movement many women who felt a sense of malaise thought of this as a unique personal problem, the emergence of women's groups has provided new interpretations. Instead of viewing their problems as a product of their inadequacies as women, wives, and mothers, women now receive support for explaining their distress as caused by existing inequalities, blocked opportunities, and exploitative role relationships. Women unhappy with their life circumstances are increasingly able to find others supporting their explanations of distress as resulting from arrangements in the family and community rather than from their own inadequacies and failures. Similar groups are emerging among the disabled, the aged, and a variety of minorities. They contend that their problems are not simply a product of their status, but of social arrangements that exacerbate their limitations. In recent years research has repeatedly demonstrated that much of the disability associated with physical and mental illness is not an inherent product of the illness but results from the manner in which the ill person responds to his condition and the manner in which it is managed. For example, much of the aggressive behavior previously associated with schizophrenia was a product of the violent way it was dealt with by the authorities rather than an inherent feature of the syndrome (Eaton and Weil 1955).

A fourth way of studying illness behavior is to examine how varying features of the health-care system influence the responses of the patient. One crucial determinant of help seeking among patients is the accessibility of medical care (Lewis, Fein, and Mechanic 1976), and barriers to care may develop because of location, financial requirements, bureaucratic responses to the patient, social distance between client and professional, and stigma in seeking assistance (Mechanic 1976a). Problems associated with inappropriate utilization can often be attacked more effectively by modifying the way agencies and professionals organize to deal with a problem than by attempting to change patient behavior.

Determinants of Illness Behavior

There are dramatic social and cultural differences in the way individuals and groups define illness and respond to symptoms. Moreover, the types of beliefs individuals have shape their responses to treatment and their cooperation with varying types of professionals. Successful treatment requires gaining the confidence of the patient, and this implies at least that the approach to treatment is not inconsistent with important social and cultural assumptions of the patient. The role of cultural differences in illness behavior is nicely illustrated by the classic study of Zborowski (1952), who described ethnic variations in responses to pain. He noted that while Jewish and Italian patients responded to pain in an emotional fashion, tending to exaggerate pain experiences, "Old Americans" tended to be more stoical and "objective," and Irish patients more frequently denied pain. In addition, while Jews and Italians had similar manifest responses to pain, their underlying attitudes tended to be different. While the Italian patients sought relief from pain and seemed satisfied when relief was obtained, the Jewish patients seemed more concerned about the significance of their pain for future health. Thus pain medication might be more effective in the former case, and reassurance about future health in the latter case.

Suchman (1964), in a study of 5,340 persons in different ethnic groups in New York City, found that ethnocentric and socially cohesive groups included more persons who knew little about disease, were skeptical toward professional medical care, and reported a dependent pattern when ill. A more recent study of a Mormon population in Utah suggests, however, that an ethnocentric and socially cohesive group that supports the use of modern medicine may encourage high acceptance and high use of medical services (Geertsen, Klauber, Rindflesh, Kane, and Gray 1975). The conclusion that one can draw from these studies is that cohesive group structures have considerable influence on members' behavior and can either assist or retard the treatment process. Such group structures can be used effectively by skilled public-health personnel to promote effective behavior, appropriate use of services, and cooperation with health-promotion programs.

Socialization of Health Attitudes and Behavior

The large range of variations in health and illness behavior from one culture to another and among varying ethnic groups suggests that these are largely learned differences, but we understand relatively little about how these patterns are taught and acquired and how the health education of children can successfully be altered. In trying to explain the cultural differences he observed, Zborowski reported that Jewish and Italian patients related that their mothers showed overprotective and overconcerned attitudes about the children's health and participation in sports, and that they were constantly warned of the advisability of avoiding colds, fights, and other threatening situations. Zborowski suggested that this overprotective attitude fostered complaining and anxieties about illness. Schachter (1959) executed an impressive series of experiments of affiliation under stress and found that firstborn and only children were more likely than others to want to be in the presence of another person when facing stress in adult life. Schachter hypothesized that the attention given to the first child and the inexperience of the parents in child rearing are likely to result in a greater dependence among such children as compared with later-born children. Consistent with Schachter's hypothesis, Tessler (1977) found in a study of 1,665 children from 587 families that early-born children were more frequent users of physician services than later-born, even controlling for variation in family size.

However simple the notion of cultural acquisition of illness behavior may appear, it is difficult to demonstrate empirically the processes of transmission. Mechanic (1964), using data acquired from 350 children and from their mothers, teachers, school records, and family illness diaries, found that the best predictors of children's illness responses were sex and age. By the fourth grade, girls were more likely to express pain and fear than boys, and these differences increased with age, although both older boys and girls were more stoical than younger children. Although the mothers' illness behavior patterns were predictive of decisions they made about the children's health, they did not successfully predict the children's response patterns. A seventeen-year follow-up of these children has now been completed, and analyses are being undertaken of the effect of childhood variables on adult health and illness behavior.

Vocabularies of Distress

It is apparent that social learning affects the vocabularies that people use to describe their problems and complaints. It is reasonable to anticipate that persons from origins in which the expression of symptoms and a desire for help are permissible will be more likely to voice such feelings than those who are socialized in cultural settings that encourage denial of such feelings. Moreover, social groups differ in the extent to which they use and accept psychological and psychodynamic vocabularies, and these are likely to shape the way people conceptualize and deal with their distress. Kadushin (1969) found, for example, that persons who were receptive to psychotherapy were part of a loose social network of friends and supporters of psychotherapy. They shared the same lifestyles, liked the same music, and had in common many social and political ideas. Such networks tend to support and encourage psychological conceptualizations of problems, just as certain families do. In contrast, other families and subgroups disapprove of such patterns of expression and tend to punish them. Zborowski (1952), for example, in describing the "Old American" family stressed the tendency of the mother to teach the child to take pain "like a man," not to be a sissy, and not to cry. Such training, he argues, does not discourage use of the doctor, but implies that such use will be based on physical needs rather than emotional concerns.

It might be anticipated that persons from subgroups that discourage the expression of psychological distress will be inhibited from showing such distress directly, but will mask it with the presentation of more acceptable symptoms. Kerckhoff and Back (1968), in a study of the diffusion among women employees of a Southern mill of a hysterical illness alleged to be caused by an unknown insect, found that the prevalence of the condition was high among women under strain who could not admit that they had a problem and who did not know how to cope with it. Bart (1968), in comparing women who entered a neurology service but who were discharged with psychiatric diagnoses with women entering a psychiatric service of the same hospital, found that they were less educated, more rural, of lower socioeconomic status, and less likely to be Jewish. Of these women, 52 percent had had a hysterectomy as compared with 21 percent of women who entered the psychiatric service. Bart suggests that such patients may be expressing psychological distress through physical attributions, thus exposing themselves to unnecessary medical procedures.

Illness Behavior as a Means of Coping

It has already been noted that psychological distress increases the probability of use of medical care. Illness behavior is part of a socially defined status and may serve as an effective means of achieving release from social expectations, as an excuse for failure, or as a way of obtaining a variety of privileges, including monetary compensation. Moreover, the physician and other health personnel may be an important source of social support and may be particularly important for patients lacking strong social ties. A vague complaint of illness may be one way of seeking reassurance and support through a recognized and socially acceptable relationship when it is difficult for the patient to confront the underlying problem in an unambiguous way without displaying weaknesses and vulnerabilities contrary to expected and learned behavior patterns. Balint (1957) and others have noted that the presenting symptoms may be of no special importance, but serve to establish the relationship between the patient and the doctor.

There are many ways in which adaptive needs interact with responses to symptoms and illness. A vast number of doctor-patient contacts involve symptoms and illnesses that are widely distributed in the population and that are more frequently untreated than treated (White, Williams, and Greenberg 1961). Thus the decision to seek care is frequently a result of contingencies surrounding the perception of symptoms. Perceptions of oneself as ill and seeking care may provide self-justification when potential failure poses much greater symbolic threats to the person's self-esteem than the process of being ill or dependent (Cole and Lejeune 1972).

A related issue is the difficulty some patients have in differentiating symptoms of psychological origin from symptoms of particular diseases. Many illnesses or medications prescribed for dealing with them produce feelings that are comparable to those associated with stress and psychopathology. Such symptoms as fatigue, restlessness, and poor appetite, for example, may result either from depression or from an acute infectious disease. When both occur concurrently, patients may attribute the effects of one to another. There is indication, for example, that long convalescence from acute infectious disease may result from the attribution of symptoms caused by depression to the acute condition (Imboden, Canter, and Cluff 1961). This complicates not only the patient's recovery but also the physician's perception and management of the patient.

Implications for Health Care

Illness behavior is a dynamic process through which the person defines problems, struggles with them, and attempts to achieve a comfortable accommodation. Such processes of adaptation are partly learned and partly shaped by the social situation and influences in the immediate environment. The health worker thus can help guide the process by suggesting constructive alternatives for the patient and by avoiding the reinforcement of distorted meanings and maladaptive responses. Treatment personnel have considerable choice as to whether they encourage realistic understanding and coping efforts among patients or whether they encourage dependence and helplessness. Much of medical care has encouraged the patient to assume a dependent stance relative to the professional and has failed to support the patient's ability to struggle for mastery over his problems. Excessive dependence and helplessness are particularly evident in chronic illness in which the degree of social disability characterizing many patients far surpasses that required by the physical condition of the patient. While the myocardial infarction patient, for example, may be troubled by the way his condition affects his ability to work and his family life, the physician frequently focuses too narrowly on minor variations in cardiac output (Aiken 1976; Reif 1975). Constructive illness behavior and the patient's coping capacities may be more influential on outcomes than many of the biological indicators on which physicians focus.

13 | The Politics of Change: The Potential for Reform

This book began by noting that both neoconservative and radical commentators on the medical-care scene share a certain pessimism about the potentials for reform. Both view interest-group politics as significant constraints on restructuring existing forms of organization or on fundamentally reshaping the delivery system. Although it would be naive to ignore the difficulties and complexities of reshaping health care in the United States, the fact remains that more progress has taken place than these critics acknowledge.

Alford (1972:164), for example, argues that change is unlikely "without the presence of a social and political movement which rejects the legitimacy of the economic and social base of pluralist politics." He maintains that barriers to reform arise from conflicts between professional monopolists who control research, teaching, and patient care and corporate rationalizers who want to extend control over the organization of care. These groups, he claims, have appropriated power over medical care with government support in a way that thwarts meeting health-care needs. Although the argument is seductive and has some elements of truth, the reality is that Alford provides no criteria by which his contention of little change in health care can be evaluated.

The evidence is, however, that considerable progress has been made in the past decade in redistributing many types of services to the poor, blacks, and other minority groups (Mechanic 1978a:198–202; Robert Wood Johnson Foundation 1978). That major problems persist is hardly a surprise; problems of distribution and fragmentation will always exist, although in altered forms. Medicine will continue to change and to offer new and expensive possibilities, and

159

new gaps in access will develop. The point is that the poor have made both relative and absolute improvements in access to care and in health-status indicators, and this is no trivial achievement. We should have ambitious ideals, even utopias. We should not be so naive, however, as to believe that we will not always fail if these are the measuring rods for progress. Ideals are essential to help us move in the directions we wish to go, but we also need more specific standards to measure our progress. Alford (1972:164) fails to inform us how we might have done better other than to indicate that government agencies should be "independent sources regulating and planning in the public interest." He fails to suggest any viable political, organizational, or technical structure that can make the necessary modifications.

Much of this book has been concerned with how we can do better in dealing with the problems of the mentally ill, other handicapped persons, and the sick aged, in enhancing relationships between patients and health practitioners, in controlling costs of medical care, in promoting our understanding of health and health behavior, and in many other areas. This broad view of problems in health care has been examined in the context of economic issues because, whether we like it or not, this is the name of the game. Although many of the ideas and recommendations suggested may not be amenable to immediate implementation, it is essential to have a long-range perspective. While policymakers often demand quick answers responsive to the pressing problems they see at the moment, the fundamental problems tend to persist, and the same issues recur year after year.

Everywhere in the world increasing costs of medical care pose serious problems. Not only has government responsibility for financing grown, but the increased costs of third-party coverage in the nongovernmental sector also impose heavy burdens on industry and limit the ability of unions to bargain for additional wages and other fringe benefits. The policymaker seeks mechanisms that will immediately allow some control over increased costs. From a short-term perspective, thus, we might focus on such matters as the best way to reimburse hospitals to increase efficiency, the value of second opinions in surgery, or the economies of physician substitution. If the innovations are successful, they can be implemented. The changes involved require no fundamental reorganization of health services, nor do they seriously threaten existing economic, political, or professional interests. Although such an emphasis contributes to cost

grams. More forceful attempts rouse fierce political conflict and rapid mobilization of opposition. When new funds are unavailable, however, and changes are desired, organizational issues must be confronted if change is to occur. Thus an effective coalition must be built among many interests. This is possible because many health-policy issues influence directly only one segment of the health field, providing a potentiality for building a coalition against the expected opposition. In recent years we have seen medical organizations break ranks on many occasions. Psychiatrists opposed the American Medical Association on staffing grants for mental-health centers, medical schools battled organized medicine on regional medical programs, hospitals fought radiologists on salaried practice, and physician groups fought each other on professional standards review organizations.

Most health agenda items are small and receive little public visibility, except among those who have a special interest in the policy. Typically, it is the special interests who monitor such legislation or administrative decisions and attempt to influence them. By bringing a wider group of political participants into such decisions—many who have opposing views but who have not been activated in the past because of lack of either organization or resources—it becomes more possible to neutralize the lobbying efforts of the special interests. One of the weaknesses of the health political scene is the lack of organization, limited resources, and modest expertise of public-interest groups (Mechanic 1978b). If better organized, they could contribute importantly to an effective coalition for change.

Such issues as national health insurance are fought more publicly, are more contentious, and have enough at stake for many groups to bring strong countervailing forces into the debate. The magnitude of the issue also ensures that the final resolution is more likely to be settled by a variety of political compromises than by technical considerations or research evidence. Because the contending interests are so diverse and the stakes are so large, such issues are usually difficult to resolve and may involve years of stalemate.

Because a major change in health policy involves many coalitions and points of cooperation, it is much easier to delay and deter a proposal through the political process than it is to innovate in any bold way. Successful innovation requires good timing and a ripe political climate, such as occurred during the New Deal or the early years of the Johnson administration, following the assassination of President Kennedy. Economic conditions are also a crucial variable, because innovation is more easily achieved when there is no threat of loss to powerful interest groups. Most of the time, however, policy efforts must be applied at the margins, leaving major new strokes for the times when special opportunities arise. Maintaining issues on the "back burners" is useful because it prepares the public and facilitates understanding of the necessary technical issues. Moreover, when the political opportunity arises the models of legislation are already available, and many of the relevant actors have already been over the details. Although it would have been unlikely that legislation affecting the safety and efficacy of drugs, for example, could have passed without the thalidomide tragedy, the previous occurrence of detailed congressional hearings and analysis set the stage for the passage of this legislation when the opportunity occurred.

Decisions in any large sector change when the environment forces adaptations. Three types of influence play a role. One major force is simply changes in buying power as reflected in the size and affluence of the population, the degree of subsidy it receives for obtaining medical services, and financial incentives implicit in health insurance programs. A second type of influence arises from the viewpoint of the public and the existing normative constraints that prescribe the way institutions must operate if they are not to violate public sensitivities. The controversies over abortion reform, Medicaid, and human experimentation illustrate such influences. Third are the various influences arising from the growth of regulatory activities and other mandated requirements over those who provide services. Medical care has always been affected to some degree by each of these types of influence, but the mix is changing, sometimes more and sometimes less rapidly.

The growth of the medical-care sector in recent decades reflects the willingness of persons and institutions to pay for such services. Such willingness is expressed in large-scale government entitlement programs, in the goals of labor to increase health-care fringe benefits in collective bargaining, and in the out-of-pocket expenditures for health insurance or medical care made by individual consumers. Although the marketplace works imperfectly, when funds become available the provision of services frequently increases. Individuals and groups, seeing that money can be made, develop the services for which funds are being provided. Thus under Medicare financing nursing-home beds have proliferated, and medical technologies have expanded enormously under the open-ended insurance arrangements characteristic of much of the American health sector.

Over time, demographic and economic changes take place that affect the purchasing power of any population group. Decision makers must adapt to these if they are to survive. With the drop in the birth rate, for example, there is lesser demand for obstetrics and pediatric care. Those practitioners and facilities providing relevant services must adapt to these changes by shifting emphases, changing location, modifying the mix of services or clients, or whatever. Thus pediatricians are increasingly giving attention to more effective primary care, social development, adolescent medicine, and the like. Similarly, hospitals in areas in which major population losses or demographic changes have taken place must eventually decide to move, consolidate, merge, change their client group, or modify their mix of services. Thus an institution providing acute medical care in a competitive environment may shift more of its focus to long-term care, home care, programs for alcoholics or drug addicts, or wherever the market has potential.

Adaptation, however, is slow, because economics is only one of many relevant factors. Adaptation requires dealing with professional ideologies, with the need for technical know-how, and with the resistance among a wide variety of actors who may find their favored routines or even their jobs at stake. Moreover, under existing financial arrangements there is considerable slack that allows efficiencies to persist, and when the crunch comes it is the weaker, less prestigious, and less politically powerful programs and institutions that fail first, while the larger and more powerful institutions take over their domain. Over time, however, the social and economic forces do produce change, and such change might be guided in a useful way by effective social and economic policy. Although we have a perception that medical institutions are intractable to external influence, the fact is that some remarkable changes have taken place. Consider some examples:

In the 1960s the problem of access to physicians was perceived as a problem of number of physicians. Thus considerable efforts were made to stimulate increases in numbers of medical graduates through developing economic incentives. Funds were provided for new medical schools, and capitation payments were made to existing schools as an incentive for increased class size. Although the initial perception was in large part faulty, the fact is that the policy worked extraordinarily well. The number of medical schools expanded, and numbers of medical graduates dramatically increased over a decade (Lewis, Fein, and Mechanic 1976). Perhaps this policy was successful because no one had anything significant to lose under existing medical-care conditions, but it is hardly an argument for the contention that change is impossible.

In the 1960s the growing imbalance between primary-care physicians and specialists became increasingly apparent. Although there was mounting concern about the inadequate number of generalists, departments of internal medicine in medical schools and, to a lesser extent, departments of pediatrics were intransigent about modifying their specialty-training orientations. Major emphasis was devoted to the training of subspecialists, with little focus on training for a more general role. Under the auspices of federal and state funding, encouragement was given for the establishment of a family-practice specialty. Although this development was not welcomed by more traditional departments in medical schools and often vigorously opposed (even sabotaged), the insistence of the public through their legislators led to the development of a vigorous family-practice program with a remarkable growth of family-practice residencies. While the early reactions of the traditional departments were disdainful, the threat of these programs contributed to their rethinking their own missions in response to the competition of family practice.

In the 1970s we are hearing a great deal from eminent professors about the general internist and pediatrician, and medical and pediatric residency training programs are shifting in their emphases. Whether this is desirable or will lead to a fundamentally different orientation to patients is not the issue. The conceptions that led to the growth of family practice as an appropriate approach to primary care or to new modes of training generalists in the basic disciplines may or may not be suitable for the future. The point is, however, that significant changes in orientation have taken place among actors who were generally viewed as having strong control over their terrains and who were not particularly anxious for such changes. Although it is too early to judge outcomes, it seems reasonable to conclude that the emergence of family practice through public efforts is having a significant influence on the way internists and pediatricians are redefining their roles.

A Note on Implementation

It is a well-known principle of politics that simply passing a law, issuing an edict, or developing a regulatory plan may have little effect on the intended targets. The development of incentives is only the first stage in a complex implementation process that may have technical as well as political uncertainties (Pressman and Wildavsky 1973). Medicine is a highly decentralized and personalized function involving hundreds of thousands of decision makers. Many doctors and other decision makers are oblivious to legislation or regulations intended to change their behavior, and such awareness is usually a prerequisite for change. Physicians are busy people and not particularly attuned to political or legislative events. Although medical organizations looking after their interests usually alert them to political developments, only a small segment of the profession gives close attention to these issues. It is quite common, therefore, for physicians not to understand the incentives that were instituted to change their "decision calculus."

Assuming that physicians understand what is expected, they may be more or less sympathetic with the goals intended. Because medicine is a highly discretionary activity governed by norms of clinical judgment, it is not too difficult to undermine or subvert incentives designed to change modes of practice. Unless the incentives are developed in an exceedingly careful way, they can be manipulated to serve the provider's interest without remedying the basic problem. Experience with modifying reimbursement and the aberrations that may result as reflected in the Medicaid mill or the gang visit (in which physicians visit patients in large groups such as nursing homes, seeing each patient briefly and billing for each) suggests that it is much easier to develop solutions in theory than to change the behavior of thousands of professionals who are extraordinarily capable of adhering to their own agendas.

Problems of Fragmentation

Much of the radical critique of the American health-care system focuses on problems of distribution of care and fragmentation. I have already noted that while a great deal is required to close gaps in access to medical care and in promoting equitable distribution, we have made significant progress in the past decade in bringing better medical care to the poor and various minority groups. Although this is no excuse to lapse in our efforts, the pessimism generated by the critical rhetoric that nothing significant is happening can also immobilize our will and commitment.

In addressing the issue of fragmentation, the critics also provide a simplistic view. No doubt we have very large problems of coordinating the complex and varied services we have developed, and it is incontestable that many disruptions of communication and continuity occur. Obviously this is a problem worthy of our attention, but we should not deceive ourselves that the continuity problem is a simple one, simply resulting from the economic and political context of our health-care system. An examination of some of the problems of continuity between general practitioners and hospitals in the English National Health Service or some of the awesome problems of bureaucratic bungling in the Communist health systems would reveal that maintaining effective continuity in light of technical and organizational complexity is a generic problem in all health-care systems. There are, of course, many aspects of the fragmentation problem that can be attacked. One important emphasis we are now promoting is the development of more primary-care physicians who take a longitudinal responsibility for the patient.

The fragmentation of the federal structure in health both reflects and contributes to fragmentation at the institutional level and at the point of delivery of care. Although in theory it would seem sensible to integrate human-services programs to simplify administrative and service-delivery programs, in practice, even if it were possible, the results might be disappointing. While an emphasis on categorical programs distorts the pattern of service delivery, providing more funds to those interests that are better organized and more vociferous, the integration of categorical interests into superagencies at the administrative level or into single-entry delivery systems at the service level not only poses problems of size but also of submergence of more specialized and less common functions to the dominant service pattern. Although categorical organization of services poses formidable problems of integration and referral, particularly in reference to multiproblem families or for patients with many medical problems, many services would be slighted if they were not organized as a special concern.

Consider the problems of depression, alcoholism, drug abuse, and general medical services. In principle, all these problems are related to general health status and should be dealt with from a single point of entry into the medical-care system. We should do much more to prepare the primary-care physician to deal with such problems, but also we had better realize that the general physician deals with a great variety of patients and is faced with considerable work pressure from a demanding patient load. The orientation of such a physician is likely to be dominated by "normal practice," and even with the best intentions he is less likely to be perceptive or knowledgeable about the handling of special areas than a practitioner specializing in these problems. Moreover, both alcoholics and drug abusers are stigmatized patients, and because of this are likely to get less sympathetic concern and attention in general medical settings as compared with more specialized programs organized around their special problems. Thus while physical malaise, depression, drinking, and drug abuse may all occur together in complex interrelationships and ideally should be dealt with in one integrated setting, these settings typically do a poor job in dealing with these more atypical problems that require different types of clinical approaches. Although some types of care, such as care for the alcoholic, might be effectively integrated into general medical practice with improved training, with specialized backup support for the primary-care physician, and with better communication with such groups as Alcoholics Anonymous, other problems are best handled in specialized settings. Among these are the problems of handicapped children, psychosis, and behavioral disabilities. Other services, such as family planning, which many physicians provide, must be supplemented by additional efforts to reach all eligible clients, particularly members of lower socioeconomic groups.

It is difficult to specify in the abstract the points at which categorical emphases should be traded for reduction of fragmentation and comprehensiveness. Certainly too great an emphasis on specialized programs results in such extensive fragmentation that it interferes in dealing with the person's or family's overall problems. Moreover, it frequently leads to duplication of effort, breakdown of communication, and conflicting advice to patients. Although comprehensiveness and integration of services are ideals to be pursued, they are extraordinarily difficult to achieve without neglecting uncommon and unique problems of patients. It is for this reason that organized groups in the community identified with a particular disease constituency continue to encourage specialized programs and categorical administrative efforts in the federal and state structures.

The Changing Culture of Medical Care

The policy issues in medical care go well beyond the problems of financing, distribution, and fragmentation. These issues arise from an enormously complex technology that is uncertain but one that also continually produces new needs and new possibilities. Although some critics see the rise of technology as an inevitable requirement of capitalist expansion and the search for new markets, others see it as a product of efforts to use science to reduce human suffering and enhance humane goals. It has become fashionable for critics to attack such new developments as coronary bypass surgery and nonintrusive body scanners. Where, they ask, is the evidence that these technologies prevent mortality and increase longevity, as if this is the only relevant consideration. Certainly there is evidence that scanners when appropriately used are an invaluable diagnostic aid, and for many patients coronary bypass surgery not only significantly reduces pain and discomfort but also greatly increases their vitality and ability to function. These are far from trivial advantages, not to be passed off by glib assertions about changes in mortality rates.

The indication is that these technologies are often used inappropriately and under circumstances in which the possible gains do not balance either the risks or the costs. This, however, is an issue of the control over technology and its appropriate use and not an issue of the value of technology itself. While it is accurate that from a world perspective such technological efforts are fantastically costly when many in the world lack the most primitive preventive and curative services, the fact is that we do not make decisions on this basis in any sector. Certainly the introduction of such technologies in poor countries is misguided when so much else is lacking, but this provides little basis for medical care decisions in the United States.

As we look to the future, the pressing need is to define the levers for constructive change and the ways to encourage them. In the present climate of increasing medical-care costs and demands for cost containment, it seems unlikely that problems of unequal access, uneven quality, and fragmented service can be dealt with largely by developing new programs and spending more money as in the past. An alternative to spending money is increased regulation, and in recent years we have witnessed a proliferation of planning attempts, performance requirements, guidelines, and auditing and review efforts. As problems continue or new ones become evident, the response is an elaboration of rules and procedures. The result is a crazy quilt of regulation that is expensive and difficult to administer and that has a deadening effect on flexibility and innovation. Such regulation is costly for those affected and requires a large pool of workers simply to comply with and monitor such compliance. Poor regulatory efforts, much like poor economic incentives, have perverse consequences and may result in behavior quite different from that desired.

Planning, of course, is intended to define problems and options clearly and to clarify the costs and benefits of varying alternatives. Just as with social policy more generally, pluralistic politics requires that planning must be approached piecemeal from the point of view of different needs, population groups, agencies, and programs. The result thus is often contradictory regulations that work at cross purposes and that often create confusion and disillusionment at the service level. There is increasing frustration with the growth of regulation in the health-care system and evidence of a growing backlash. It seems fairly clear that the core problems we face in health care are unlikely to be solved simply by more and more rule making.

The broad goal of cost containment within the context of an equitable and comprehensive health-care system defined in the introduction of this book requires change in normative conceptions. It requires new social definitions of the value and limitations of medical care and of the role of individuals and social groups in maintaining and reinforcing good health. It requires a new consensus that places emphasis on new goals for health care and priority on maintaining industrial and community conditions that contain environmental threats to health. It requires tremendous pressure on health professionals and health institutions by the organized consumer groups and representatives of labor, industry, and government who must assume the costs for inefficient and dysfunctional developments in the health-care sector.

Ideological and cultural forces have been extraordinarily important in shaping medical organization and patients' responses to the care they receive. Cultural conceptions define the ways people deal with personal and group distress, their views on and management of the problems of birth and death, and the relationships between the medical sector and failures in functioning. They define what are acceptable uses of the physician and the range of appropriate practitioners for dealing with the great variety of human maladies. In short, the future of medicine and the functions it plays in human society will be a product of the ways in which it is defined.

I do not suggest that such a reformulation is either easy or probable. The strength of existing conceptions, the dominance of existing institutions and practitioners, the inertia of the public, and the costs of organizing and giving attention to these matters are all significant impediments to change. We also lack knowledge and experience in developing functional substitutes for medical care and in convincing the public of their value. Indeed, change when it does occur is most likely to come in those areas in which the forces of new knowledge, economics, and ideology converge.

Two relatively recent "revolutions" in health care are instructive. In the case of birth control the development of new technology—the pill—occurred in a context in which there was increasing concern about the growth of population and changes in family ideas about the number of children desired and sex roles. The pill provided a relatively simple opportunity to exercise control over family size, while economic and cultural conceptions provided the motivation to do so. Because of the growth of concern about population size and attendant problems, social policy tended to support the diffusion of the pill and also made abortion and sterilization more acceptable and available modes of controlling fertility.

Perhaps the largest change in recent decades in the health field came with the deinstitutionalization of the mentally ill. Although deinstitutionalization has obvious problems, as discussed in this book, it constitutes a remarkable shift in patterns of care within a relatively short period. The incentive for deinstitutionalization came from growing economic problems in retaining large numbers of patients in mental hospitals and the need on the part of states for relief of this cost burden. Social-science and civil-liberties concerns provided the ideology that justified the retention of large numbers of mental patients in the community, and the development of the psychoactive drugs provided a means for some control over the most bizarre manifestations of mental illness, giving administrators, mental-health personnel, and families more confidence in their ability to deal with the change. The development of welfare policy further provided the economic means to support those patients in the community who had no other source of economic subsistence. No single aspect of this process was sufficient in itself; it was the convergence of these forces that produced the remarkable changes that occurred.

We have no way of knowing what developments in knowledge and technology will allow further dramatic shifts in the future. The history of such institutions as tuberculosis sanatoriums, large mental hospitals, and artificial lung units for polio victims suggests that changes in knowledge and technology, environmental conditions, and

25: 417–52. Palo Alto, Calif.: Annual Reviews, Inc.

Dohrenwend, Bruce P., and Barbara Snell Dohrenwend. 1969. *Social Status and Psychological Disorder: A Causal Inquiry.* New York: Wiley-Interscience.

Donabedian, Avedis. 1965. *A Review of Some Experiences with Prepaid Group Practice.* Ann Arbor: University of Michigan School of Public Health, Research Series No. 12.

Downs, Anthony. 1967. *Inside Bureaucracy.* Boston: Little, Brown.

Duff, Raymond S., and August B. Hollingshead. 1968. *Sickness and Society.* New York: Harper & Row.

Durkheim, Emile. 1951. *Suicide: A Study in Sociology.* Edited and with an introduction by George Simpson. New York: The Free Press.

Eaton, Joseph W., and Robert J. Weil. 1955. *Culture and Mental Disorders: A Comparative Study of the Hutterites and Other Populations.* New York: The Free Press.

Enthoven, Alain C. 1978a. "Consumer-Choice Health Plan. Inflation and Inequity in Health Care Today: Alternatives for Cost Control and an Analysis of Proposals for National Health Insurance." *New England Journal of Medicine* 298 (March 23): 650–58.

Enthoven, Alain C. 1978b. "Consumer-Choice Health Plan. A National-Health-Insurance Proposal Based on Regulated Competition in the Private Sector." *New England Journal of Medicine* 298 (March 30): 709–20.

Enthoven, Alain C. 1977. "National Health Insurance," memorandum for Department of Health, Education and Welfare Secretary Joseph Califano.

Fairweather, George. 1978. "The Development, Evaluation, and Diffusion of Rehabilitative Programs: A Social Change Process," pp. 295–308 in Leonard I. Stein and Mary Ann Test, eds., *Alternatives to Mental Hospital Treatment.* New York: Plenum.

Farquhar, John W., Peter D. Wood, Henry Breitrose, William L. Haskell, Anthony J. Meyer, Nathan Maccoby, Janet K. Alexander, Byron W. Brown, Jr., Alfred L. McAlister, Joyce D. Nash, and Michael P. Stern. 1977. "Community Education for Cardiovascular Health." *Lancet* 1 (June 4): 1192–95.

Follette, William, and Nicholas A. Cummings. 1968. "Psychiatric Services and Medical Utilization in a Prepaid Health Plan Setting," part II. *Medical Care* 6:31–41.

Follette, William, and Nicholas A. Cummings. 1967. "Psychiatric Services and Medical Utilization in a Prepaid Health Plan Setting." *Medical Care* 5 (January–February): 25–35.

Follman, J. F., Jr. 1970. *Insurance Coverage for Mental Illness.* New York: American Management Association.

Freidson, Eliot. 1975. *Doctoring Together: A Study of Professional Social Control.* New York: Elsevier.

Freidson, Eliot. 1970a. *Profession of Medicine: A Study of the Sociology of Applied Knowledge.* New York: Dodd, Mead.

Freidson, Eliot. 1970b. *Professional Dominance: The Social Structure of Medical Care.* New York: Atherton.

Freidson, Eliot. 1960. "Client Control and Medical Practice." *American Journal of Sociology* 65 (January): 374–82.

Fried, Charles. 1975. "Rights and Health Care—Beyond Equity and Efficiency." *New England Journal of Medicine* 293 (July 31): 241–45.

Friedman, Lawrence M. 1971. "The Idea of Right as a Social and Legal Concept." *Journal of Social Issues* 27: 189–98.

Friedman, Lawrence M. 1969. "Social Welfare Legislation: An Introduction." *Stanford Law Review* 21 (January): 217–47.

Friedman, Lawrence M. 1968. *Government and Slum Housing: A Century of Frustration.* Chicago: Rand McNally.

Friedman, Meyer, and Ray H. Rosenman. 1974. *Type A Behavior and Your Heart.* New York: Alfred A. Knopf.

Fuchs, Victor R. 1974. *Who Shall Live? Health, Economics, and Social Choice.* New York: Basic Books.

Fuchs, Victor R. 1968. "The Growing Demand for Medical Care." *New England Journal of Medicine* 279 (July 25): 190–95.

Fullerton, Donald T., Francis N. Lohrenz, and Gregory R. Nycz. 1976. "Utilization of Prepaid Services by Patients with Psychiatric Diagnoses." *American Journal of Psychiatry* 133 (September): 1057–60.

Gardner, Elmer A. 1974. "Implications of Psychoactive Drug Therapy." Editorial, *New England Journal of Medicine* 290 (April 4): 800–801.

Geertsen, Reed, Melville R. Klauber, Mark Rindflesh, Robert L. Kane, and Robert Gray, 1975. "A Re-Examination of Suchman's Views on Social Factors in Health Care Utilization." *Journal of Health and Social Behavior* 16 (June): 226–37.

Ginzberg, Eli. 1977. *The Limits of Health Reform: The Search for Realism.* New York: Basic Books.

Glaser, William A. 1970. *Paying the Doctor: Systems of Remuneration and Their Effects.* Baltimore: Johns Hopkins Press.

Glass, Albert J. 1958. "Observations upon the Epidemiology of Mental Illness in Troops During Warfare," pp. 185–98 in *Symposium on Preventive and Social Psychiatry.* Washington, D.C.: Walter Reed Army Institute of Research, U.S. Government Printing Office.

Glasscote, Raymond M., Jon Gudeman, and Donald G. Miles. 1977. *Creative Mental Health Services for the Elderly.* Washington, D.C.: American Psychiatric Association.

Goldberg, Irving D., Goldie Krantz, and Ben Z. Locke. 1970. "Effect of a

Short-term Outpatient Psychiatric Therapy Benefit on the Utilization of Medical Services in a Prepaid Group Practice Medical Program." *Medical Care* 8 (September–October): 419–28.

Greenley, James R., and David Mechanic. 1976. "Social Selection in Seeking Help for Psychological Problems." *Journal of Health and Social Behavior* 17 (September): 249–62.

Grossman, Michael. 1972. *The Demand for Health: A Theoretical and Empirical Investigation.* National Bureau of Economic Research Occasional Paper Series, No. 119. New York: Columbia University Press.

Gurin, Gerald, Joseph Veroff, and Sheila Feld. 1960. *Americans View Their Mental Health.* New York: Basic Books.

Haggerty, Robert J. 1977. "Changing Lifestyles to Improve Health." *Preventive Medicine* 6 (June): 276–89.

Haggerty, Robert J., Klaus J. Roghmann, and Ivan B. Pless. 1975. *Child Health and the Community.* New York: Wiley-Interscience.

Havighurst, Clark C. 1977. "Controlling Health Care Costs: Strengthening the Private Sector's Hand." *Journal of Health Politics, Policy and Law* 1 (Winter): 471–98.

Havighurst, Clark C. 1973. "Regulation of Health Facilities and Services by 'Certificate of Need.' " *Virginia Law Review* 59 (October): 1143–1232.

Hetherington, Robert W., Carl E. Hopkins, and Milton I. Roemer. 1975. *Health Insurance Plans: Promise and Performance.* New York: Wiley-Interscience.

Illich, Ivan. 1976. *Medical Nemesis: The Expropriation of Health.* New York: Pantheon.

Imboden, John B., Arthur Canter, and Leighton Cluff. 1961. "Symptomatic Recovery from Medical Disorders." *Journal of the American Medical Association* 178 (December 30): 1182–84.

Institute of Medicine. 1975. *Legalized Abortion and the Public Health,* a policy statement by a Committee of the Institute of Medicine. Washington, D.C.: National Academy of Sciences.

Institute of Medicine. 1973. *A Strategy for Evaluating Health Services: Contrasts in Health Status,* vol. 2. Washington, D.C.: National Academy of Sciences.

Janis, Irving L., and Seymour Feshbach. 1953. "Effects of Fear-Arousing Communications." *Journal of Abnormal and Social Psychology* 48 (January): 78–92.

Janis, Irving L., and Leon Mann. 1977. *Decision Making: A Psychological Analysis of Conflict, Choice, and Commitment.* New York: The Free Press.

Jenkins, C. David. 1976. "Recent Evidence Supporting Psychologic and Social Risk Factors for Coronary Disease," part II. *New England Journal of Medicine* 294 (May 6): 1033–38.

Kadushin, Charles. 1969. *Why People Go to Psychiatrists.* New York: Atherton.

Kagan, Jerome. 1976. "Resilience and Continuity in Psychological Development," pp. 97–121 in Ann M. Clarke and A. D. B. Clarke, eds., *Early Experience: Myth and Evidence.* New York: The Free Press.

Katz, Harvey P., and Robert R. Clancy. 1974. "Accuracy of a Home Throat Culture Program: A Study of Parent Participation in Health Care." *Pediatrics* 53 (May): 687–91.

Kerckhoff, Alan C., and Kurt W. Back. 1968. *The June Bug: A Study of Hysterical Contagion.* New York: Appleton-Century-Crofts.

Klarman, Herbert E., 1965. *The Economics of Health.* New York: Columbia University Press.

Knowles, John H. 1977a. "The Responsibility of the Individual." *Daedalus* 106 (Winter): 57–80.

Knowles, John H., ed. 1977b. "Doing Better and Feeling Worse: Health in the United States." *Daedalus* 106 (Winter): entire issue.

Lasagna, Louis. 1970. "Physicians' Behavior Toward the Dying Patient," pp. 83–101 in Orville G. Brim, Jr., Howard E. Freeman, Sol Levine, and Norman A. Scotch, eds., *The Dying Patient.* New York: Russell Sage Foundation.

Last, J. M. 1977. "Health-Service Research—Does It Make a Difference?" Letter to the editor, *New England Journal of Medicine* 297 (November 10): 1073.

Lave, Lester B., and Eugene P. Seskin. 1970. "Air Pollution and Human Health." *Science* 169 (August 21): 723–33.

Leaf, Philip J. 1978. "Legal Intervention into a Mental Health System: The Outcomes of *Wyatt* v. *Stickney.*" Ph.D. dissertation, Department of Sociology, University of Wisconsin, Madison.

Lewis, Charles E. 1977. "Health-Services Research and Innovations in Health-Care Delivery: Does Research Make a Difference?" *New England Journal of Medicine* 297 (August 25): 423–27.

Lewis, Charles E., Rashi Fein, and David Mechanic. 1976. *A Right to Health: The Problem of Access to Primary Medical Care.* New York: Wiley-Interscience.

Lewis, Charles E., and Harold W. Keairnes. 1970. "Controlling Costs of Medical Care by Expanding Insurance Coverage: Study of a Paradox." *New England Journal of Medicine* 282 (June 18): 1405–12.

Lewis, Charles E., and Mary Ann Lewis. 1977. "The Potential Impact of Sexual Equality on Health." *New England Journal of Medicine* 297 (October 20): 863–69.

Lewis, Charles E., and Mary Ann Lewis. 1974. "The Impact of Television Commercials on Health-Related Beliefs and Behaviors of Children." *Pediatrics* 53 (March): 431–35.

Lewis, Charles E., Mary Ann Lewis, Ann Lorimer, and Beverly B. Palmer. 1975. *Child-Initiated Care: A Study of the Determinants of Illness Behavior of*

Children. Los Angeles: University of California Center for Health Sciences.

Leventhal, Howard. 1970. "Findings and Theory in the Study of Fear Communications," pp. 119–86 in Leonard Berkowitz, ed., *Advances in Experimental Social Psychology,* vol. 5. New York: Academic Press.

Ley, P., and M. S. Spelman. 1967. *Communicating with the Patient.* London: Staples Press.

Linn, Lawrence S. 1968. "The Mental Hospital in the Patient's Phenomenal World." Ph.D. dissertation, Department of Sociology, University of Wisconsin, Madison.

Logan, R. F. L. 1971. "National Health Planning—An Appraisal of the State of the Art." *International Journal of Health Services* 1 (February): 6–17.

Lynch, James J. 1977. *The Broken Heart: The Medical Consequences of Loneliness.* New York: Basic Books.

Maddox, George L. 1962. "Some Correlates of Differences in Self-Assessment of Health Status Among the Elderly." *Journal of Gerontology* 17 (April): 180–85.

McKeown, Thomas. 1976. *The Role of Medicine: Dream, Mirage, or Nemesis?* London: Nuffield Provincial Hospitals Trust.

McKeown, Thomas, ed. 1968. *Screening in Medical Care: Reviewing the Evidence.* London: Oxford University Press.

Mechanic, David. 1978a. *Medical Sociology.* 2d ed. New York: The Free Press.

Mechanic, David. 1978b. "The Medical Marketplace and Public Interest Law: Part I. The Medical Marketplace and Its Delivery Failures," pp. 350–74 in Burton A. Weisbrod in collaboration with Joel F. Handler and Neil K. Komesar, *Public Interest Law: An Economic and Institutional Analysis.* Berkeley: University of California Press.

Mechanic, David. 1978c. "Alternatives to Mental Hospital Treatment: A Sociological Perspective," pp. 309–20 in Leonard I. Stein and Mary Ann Test, eds., *Alternatives to Mental Hospital Treatment.* New York: Plenum Press.

Mechanic, David. 1978d. "Considerations in the Design of Mental Health Benefits under National Health Insurance." *American Journal of Public Health* 68 (May): 482–88.

Mechanic, David. 1977a. "The Growth of Medical Technology and Bureaucracy: Implications for Medical Care." *Milbank Memorial Fund Quarterly (Health and Society)* 55 (Winter): 61–78.

Mechanic, David. 1977b. "Illness Behavior, Social Adaptation, and the Management of Illness: A Comparison of Educational and Medical Models." *Journal of Nervous and Mental Disease* 165 (August): 79–87.

Mechanic, David. 1976a. *The Growth of Bureaucratic Medicine: An Inquiry into the Dynamics of Patient Behavior and the Organization of Medical Care.* New York: Wiley-Interscience.

Mechanic, David. 1976b. "Sex, Illness, Illness Behavior, and the Use of Health

Services." *Journal of Human Stress* 2 (December): 29–40.

Mechanic, David. 1976c. "Stress, Illness, and Illness Behavior." *Journal of Human Stress* 2 (June): 2–6.

Mechanic, David. 1976d. "Rationing Health Care: Public Policy and the Medical Marketplace." *Hastings Center Report* 6 (February): 34–37.

Mechanic, David. 1976e. "Some Social Aspects of the Medical Malpractice Dilemma." *Duke Law Journal* 1975 (January): 1179–96.

Mechanic, David. 1975. "The Organization of Medical Practice and Practice Orientations among Physicians in Prepaid and Nonprepaid Primary Care Settings." *Medical Care* 13 (March): 189–204.

Mechanic, David. 1974a. "Patient Behavior and the Organization of Medical Care," pp. 67–85 in Laurence R. Tancredi, ed., *Ethics of Health Care.* Washington, D.C.: National Academy of Sciences.

Mechanic, David. 1974b. "Social Structure and Personal Adaptation: Some Neglected Dimensions," pp. 32–44 in George V. Coelho, David A. Hamburg, and John E. Adams, eds., *Coping and Adaptation.* New York: Basic Books.

Mechanic, David. 1973. "The Sociology of Organizations," pp. 138–66 in Saul Feldman, ed., *The Administration of Mental Helath Services.* Springfield, Ill.: Charles C. Thomas.

Mechanic, David. 1972a. *Public Expectations and Health Care: Essays on the Changing Organization of Health Services.* New York: Wiley-Interscience.

Mechanic, David. 1972b. "General Medical Practice: Some Comparisons between the Work of Primary Care Physicians in the United States and England and Wales." *Medical Care* 10 (September–October): 402–20.

Mechanic, David. 1972c. "Social Psychologic Factors Affecting the Presentation of Bodily Complaints." *New England Journal of Medicine* 286 (May 25): 1132–39.

Mechanic, David. 1969. *Mental Health and Social Policy.* Englewood Cliffs, N.J.: Prentice-Hall.

Mechanic, David. 1964. "The Influence of Mothers on Their Children's Health Attitudes and Behavior." *Pediatrics* 33 (March): 444–53.

Mechanic, David, and Richard Tessler. 1973. "Comparison of Consumer Response to Prepaid Group Practice and Alternative Insurance Plans in Milwaukee County: A Preliminary Report." Publication 5–73, Research and Analytic Report Series, Center for Medical Sociology and Health Services Research, University of Wisconsin, Madison.

Milgram, Stanley. 1974. *Obedience to Authority: An Experimental View.* New York: Harper & Row.

Miller, Neal E. 1975. "Applications of Learning and Biofeedback to Psychiatry and Medicine," pp. 349–65 in Alfred M. Freedman, Harold I. Kaplan, and Benjamin J. Sadock, eds., *Comprehensive Textbook of Psychiatry,* vol. 1. 2d ed. Baltimore: Williams and Wilkins.

Murphy, George E. 1975a. "The Physician's Responsibility for Suicide: I. An Error of Commission." *Annals of Internal Medicine* 82 (March): 301-304.

Murphy, George E. 1975b. "The Physician's Responsibility for Suicide: II. Errors of Omission." *Annals of Internal Medicine* 82 (March): 305-309.

National Commission for Manpower Policy. 1976. *Employment Impacts of Health Policy Developments,* Special Report No. 11. Washington, D.C.: Government Printing Office.

National Research Council. 1977. *Personnel Needs and Training for Biomedical and Behavioral Research, 1977 Report,* vol. 1. Washington, D.C.: National Academy of Sciences.

Palmore, Erdman, and Clark Luikart. 1972. "Health and Social Factors Related to Life Satisfaction." *Journal of Health and Social Behavior* 13 (March): 68-80.

Parry, Hugh J., Mitchell B. Balter, Glen D. Mellinger, Ira H. Cisin, and Dean I. Manheimer. 1973. "National Patterns of Psychotherapeutic Drug Use." *Archives of General Psychiatry* 28 (June): 769-83.

Patrick, Donald L., Jeff Eagle, and Jules V. Coleman. 1978. "Primary Care Treatment of Emotional Problems in an HMO." *Medical Care* 16 (January): 47-60.

Perkoff, Gerald T., Lawrence Kahn, and Phillip J. Haas. 1976. "The Effects of an Experimental Prepaid Group Practice on Medical Care Utilization and Cost." *Medical Care* 14 (May): 432-49.

Pressman, Jeffrey L., and Aaron Wildavsky. 1973. *Implementation: How Great Expectations in Washington Are Dashed in Oakland; Or, Why It's Amazing that Federal Programs Work at All, This Being a Saga of the Economic Development Administration as Told by Two Sympathetic Observers Who Seek to Build Morals on a Foundation of Ruined Hopes.* Berkeley: University of California Press.

Rabin, D., and K. Spector. 1977. *Factors That Affect New Practitioner Performance in Practice Setting.* Physician Assistant/Nurse Practitioner Manpower Symposium, Airlie House, Airlie, Virginia.

Reed, Louis S., Evelyn S. Myers, and Patricia L. Scheidemandel. 1972. *Health Insurance and Psychiatric Care: Utilization and Cost.* Washington, D.C.: American Psychiatric Association.

Reif, Laura Jean. 1975. "Cardiacs and Normals: The Social Construction of a Disability." Ph.D. dissertation, University of California, San Francisco.

Reinhardt, Uwe E. 1975. *Physician Productivity and the Demand for Health Manpower: An Economic Analysis.* Cambridge, Mass.: Ballinger.

Reinholds, Harold. 1976. *Hospital Incentive Reimbursement: An Institutional Overview.* Studies in Welfare Policy No. 9. Lansing, Mich.: Michigan Department of Social Services.

Reynolds, Lloyd G. 1976. *Microeconomics: Analysis and Policy.* Rev. ed.

Homewood, Ill.: Richard Irwin.

Richards, N. David. 1975. "Methods and Effectiveness of Health Education: The Past, Present and Future of Social Scientific Involvement." *Social Science and Medicine* 9 (March): 141-56.

Robert Wood Johnson Foundation. 1978. *America's Health Care System: A Comprehensive Portrait.* Special Report No. 1, Princeton, N.J.

Robertson, Leon S. 1976. "Estimates of Motor Vehicle Seat Belt Effectiveness and Use: Implications for Occupant Crash Protection." *American Journal of Public Health* 66 (September): 859-64.

Robertson, Leon S. 1975. "Behavioral Research and Strategies in Public Health: A Demur." *Social Science and Medicine* 9 (March): 165-70.

Robins, Lee N. 1966. *Deviant Children Grown Up: A Sociological and Psychiatric Study of Sociopathic Personality.* Baltimore: Williams and Wilkins.

Rogers, Everett M. 1962. *Diffusion of Innovations.* New York: The Free Press.

Rosengren, William R., and Mark Lefton, eds. 1970. *Organizations and Clients: Essays in the Sociology of Service.* Columbus, Ohio: Charles E. Merrill.

Rosenhan, D. L. 1973. "On Being Sane in Insane Places." *Science* 179 (January 19): 250-58.

Rosenstock, Irwin M. 1969. "Prevention of Illness and Maintenance of Health," pp. 168-90 in John Kosa, Aaron Antonovsky, and Irving Kenneth Zola, eds., *Poverty and Health: A Sociological Analysis.* Cambridge: Harvard University Press.

Rosenstock, Irwin M. 1960. "What Research in Motivation Suggests for Public Health." *American Journal of Public Health* 50 (March): 295-302.

Sarason, Seymour B. 1972. *The Creation of Settings and the Future Societies.* San Francisco: Jossey-Bass.

Schachter, Stanley. 1959. *The Psychology of Affiliation: Experimental Studies of the Sources of Gregariousness.* Stanford: Stanford University Press.

Scull, Andrew T. 1977. *Decarceration: Community Treatment and the Deviant.* Englewood Cliffs, N.J.: Prentice-Hall.

Segal, Steven P., and Uri Aviram. 1978. *The Mentally Ill in Community-Based Sheltered Care: A Study of Community Care and Social Integration.* New York: Wiley-Interscience.

Seligman, Martin E. P. 1975. *Helplessness: On Depression, Development, and Death.* San Francisco: W. H. Freeman.

Shepherd, Michael, Brian Cooper, Alexander C. Brown, and Graham Kalton. 1966. *Psychiatric Illness in General Practice.* London: Oxford University Press.

Silver, Laurens H. 1974. "The Legal Accountability of Nonprofit Hospitals," pp. 183-200 in Clark C. Havighurst, ed., *Regulating Health Facilities Construction.* Washington, D.C.: American Enterprise Institute for Public Policy Research.

Simmons, Roberta G., Susan D. Klein, and Richard L. Simmons. 1977. *Gift of Life: The Social and Psychological Impact of Organ Transplantation.* New York: Wiley-Interscience.

Smits, Helen, and Peter Draper. 1974. "Care of the Aged: An English Lesson?" *Annals of Internal Medicine* 80 (June): 747–53.

Steele, James L., and William H. McBroom. 1972. "Conceptual and Empirical Dimensions of Health Behavior." *Journal of Health and Social Behavior* 13 (December): 382–92.

Stein, Leonard I., and Mary Ann Test, eds. 1978. *Alternatives to Mental Hospital Treatment.* New York: Plenum Press.

Stein, Leonard I., and Mary Ann Test. 1976. "Training in Community Living: One-Year Evaluation." *American Journal of Psychiatry* 133 (August): 917–18.

Stotsky, Bernard A. 1970. *The Nursing Home and the Aged Psychiatric Patient.* New York: Appleton-Century-Crofts.

Strauss, Anselm L. 1969. "Medical Organization, Medical Care and Lower Income Groups." *Social Science and Medicine* 3 (August): 143–77.

Stunkard, Albert J. 1976. *The Pain of Obesity.* Palo Alto: Bull Publishing.

Suchman, Edward A. 1964. "Sociomedical Variations among Ethnic Groups." *American Journal of Sociology* 70 (November): 319–31.

Sudnow, David. 1967. *Passing On: The Social Organization of Dying.* Englewood Cliffs, N.J.: Prentice-Hall.

Szasz, Thomas S. 1974. *The Myth of Mental Illness: Foundations of a Theory of Personal Conduct.* Rev. ed. New York: Harper & Row.

Tessler, Richard. 1977. "Family Structure and Children's Use of Medical Services: A Research Note." Unpublished manuscript, University of Massachusetts.

Tessler, Richard, and David Mechanic. 1978. "Psychological Distress and Perceived Health Status." *Journal of Health and Social Behavior* 19 (September): 254–62.

Tessler, Richard, and David Mechanic. 1975. "Factors Affecting the Choice between Prepaid Group Practice and Alternative Insurance Programs." *Milbank Memorial Fund Quarterly (Health and Society)* 53 (Spring): 149–72.

Tessler, Richard, David Mechanic, and Margaret Dimond. 1976. "The Effect of Psychological Distress on Physician Utilization: A Prospective Study." *Journal of Health and Social Behavior* 17 (December): 353–64.

Thomas, Lewis. 1977. "On the Science and Technology of Medicine." *Daedalus* 106 (Winter): 35–46.

Titmuss, Richard M. 1971. *The Gift Relationship: From Human Blood to Social Policy.* New York: Pantheon.

Townsend, Peter. 1962. *The Last Refuge: A Survey of Residential Institutions and Homes for the Aged in England and Wales.* London: Routledge & Kegan Paul.

U.S. Department of Health, Education, and Welfare, 1977. *Health: United States, 1976-1977, Chartbook.* Washington, D.C.: Government Printing Office.

U.S. Health Resources Administration, National Center for Health Statistics, 1975. *Health Resources Statistics: Health Manpower and Health Facilities.* Washington, D.C.: Government Printing Office.

U.S. National Institute of Mental Health, Division of Biometry and Epidemiology. 1976. *Deinstitutionalization: An Analytic Review and Sociological Perspective,* Series D, No. 4. Washington, D.C.: Government Printing Office.

U.S. President's Commission on Mental Health. 1978. *Task Panel Reports Submitted to the President's Commission,* vol. 2 (Report of the Task Panel on the Nature and Scope of the Problem). Washington, D.C.: Government Printing Office.

U.S. President's Commission on Mental Health. 1977. *Preliminary Report to the President.* Washington, D.C.

U.S. President's Science Advisory Committee Panel. 1972. *Improving Health Care Through Research and Development.* Washington, D.C.: Government Printing Office.

Warner, Kenneth E. 1977. "The Effects of the Anti-Smoking Campaign on Cigarette Consumption." *American Journal of Public Health* 67 (July): 645-50.

Weisbrod, Burton A., Mary Ann Test, and Leonard I. Stein. 1977. "An Alternative to the Mental Hospital: Benefits and Costs." Unpublished manuscript, Department of Economics, University of Wisconsin, Madison.

Weissman, Myrna M., and Gerald L. Klerman. 1977. "Sex Differences and the Epidemiology of Depression." *Archives of General Psychiatry* 34 (January): 98-111.

White, Kerr L., T. Franklin Williams, and Bernard G. Greenberg. 1961. "The Ecology of Medical Care." *New England Journal of Medicine* 265 (November 2): 885-92.

Williams, Allan F., and Henry Wechsler. 1972. "Interrelationship of Preventive Actions in Health and Other Areas." *Health Services Reports* 87 (December): 969-76.

Wing, J. K. 1967. "The Modern Management of Schizophrenia," pp. 3-28 in Hugh Freeman and James Farndale, eds., *New Aspects of the Mental Health Services.* New York: Pergamon Press.

Wing, J. K. 1962. "Institutionalism in Mental Hospitals." *British Journal of Social and Clinical Psychology* 1 (February): 38-51.

Worthington, William, and Laurens H. Silver. 1970. "Regulation of Quality of Care in Hospitals: The Need for Change." *Law and Contemporary Problems* 35 (Spring): 305-33.

Zborowski, Mark. 1952. "Cultural Components in Responses to Pain." *Journal of Social Issues* 8:16-30.

Index

Abortion, 110, 166
Accident field, 139
Accountability, 117–21
Adolescents, 33, 34–36
Advertising, 39, 43–44
Aiken, Linda H., 52, 159, 160
Alcohol, Drug Abuse, and Mental
    Health Administration, 162
Alcoholics Anonymous, 171
Alcoholism, 27, 28, 30, 33, 82, 83,
    170–71
Alford, Robert R., 159, 160
Alienation, 80, 148
Allen, Priscilla, 70
Allocation of health care, 3–5, 20–21;
    see also Rationing
Ambivalence toward physicians, 36
Ambulatory care, 15, 93, 94, 137
American Medical Association, 165
American Psychological Association,
    77
Amphetamines, 81
Analytic research, 128, 131-32
Anxiety, 16, 32, 80, 82, 142
Apathy syndrome, 54
Apple, Dorrian, 148
Andersen, Ronald, 80
Arrow, Kenneth J., 38, 93
Artificial kidney, 175
Attribution approaches, 142
Autopsy, 115, 116
Aviram, Uri, 67, 72, 144
Avnet, Helen Hershfield, 76, 77

Back, Kurt W., 156
Balint, Michael, 41, 156
Balter, Mitchell B., 81

Barbiturates, 81
Bart, Pauline B., 156
Bauman, Barbara, 148
Becker, Marshall H., 31, 149
Beeson, Paul B., 15
Behavior modification, 18, 37
Behavioral research, 137–45; see also
    Health and illness behavior
Biofeedback, 142, 144
Bipolar depression, 83
Birth control, 174
Board and care facilities, 66, 70, 144
Body scanners, nonintrusive, 172
Bone, Margaret, 152
Brenner, M. Harvey, 140
British National Health Service, 8, 59,
    96, 100, 170
Brook, Robert H., 15, 42
Brown, Alexander C., 80
Brown, Bertram, 77, 78
Brown, G. W., 152
Bureaucracy, 8
Burn treatment, 175

Canter, Arthur, 156
Capitation programs, 19, 20, 57, 59,
    60, 69, 85, 98
Categorical grants, 69
Center for Health Services
    Administration, University of
    Chicago, 130
Certificates of need, 7
Children, health behavior of, 33–35
Chronic diseases: see Long-term care
Cisin, Ira H., 81
Clancy, Robert R., 37
Cluff, Leighton, 156

Cobb, Sidney, 141
Cochrane, A. L., 4
Coinsurance, 19, 76, 77, 84, 93
Cole, Stephen, 156
Coleman, Jules V., 82
Collective bargaining, 162, 166
College students, 35–36
Combat stress reactions, 152
Community, concept of, 73–74
Community care programs, 54, 55, 61, 64–74, 152
Community mental-health centers, 69
Community prevention, 18
Competition, 45, 47
Consent, 115–117, 120
Consumer choice, 38–47
Consumer Choice Health Plan, 39
Consumer sovereignty, 39, 46
Consumption of services, cost containment and, 11–14
Convalescence, 156
Cooper, Brian, 80
Cooper, Michael H., 21, 100
Coping strategy, 32, 156–57
Coronary bypass surgery, 51, 172
Cost containment, 8, 10–22
    alternatives to existing patterns, 15–18
    factors affecting consumption of services, 11–14
    factors affecting production of services, 14–15
    health-services research and, 18–19
    rationing: *see* Rationing
Cost sharing, 19, 38, 39, 76, 77, 84, 92–95, 161
Crawford, Robert, 25
Cummings, Nicholas A., 84, 87

Dalison, Bridgit, 152
Daughety, Virginia S., 80
Davis, Ann E., 88
Davis, Karen, 100, 109
Day care, 59
Deductibles, 19, 76, 77, 84, 93
Defense, Department of, 161, 162
Deinstitutionalization, 64–74, 144, 174
Demonstration projects, 125, 128, 134–36
Denial, 32
Dependence, 36

Depression, 16, 17, 80–84, 142, 143, 148, 170–71
Diabetes, 144
Dimond, Margaret, 80, 148
Dinitz, Simon, 88
Discrimination, 107, 109–11
Distress, 147, 148, 155–56
Dohrenwend, Barbara Snell, 77, 148
Dohrenwend, Bruce P., 77, 148
Donabedian, Avedis, 45
Downs, Anthony, 56
Draper, Peter, 59
Drinking, 27, 28, 30, 33, 82, 83, 170–71
Drug abuse, 33, 83, 137, 139, 170–71
Drugs, regulation of, 28–29, 162, 166
Duff, Raymond S., 116
Durkheim, Emile, 140

Eagle, Jeff, 82
Eaton, Joseph W., 66, 153
Elderly, 5, 17–18
    long-term care and: *see* Long-term care
    nursing homes, 17, 54, 56, 58–60, 65, 70, 144
    in population, 54–55
Energy crisis, 28
Enthoven, Alain C., 39, 45
Ethical issues, 104–21
    approaches to accountability, 117–21
    autopsy, 115, 116
    conflicts in values, expectations, and incentives, 112–13
    consent, 115–17, 120
    inequalities between providers and patients, 113–15
    organ donation, 115, 116
    professional behavior of providers, 107–109
    rationing: *see* Rationing
Evaluation research, 132–33
Exercise, 26, 27–28, 32, 137
Expectations, 13, 16, 112–13
Explicit rationing, 20, 21, 98–101
Extrainstitutional pressures on health-care programs, 117, 120

Fair market test, 38
Fairweather, George, 62

Family planning, 171
Family-practice program, 168
Farquhar, John W., 12, 26
Fatigue, 147
Fear, 32
Federal government, 5, 6, 161-63
Fee-for-service plans, 84-85, 112-13
Fee listings, 43-44, 45
Fein, Rashi, 6, 79, 129, 153, 167
Feshbach, Seymour, 32
Fixed prospective budgeting, 19, 20
Follette, William, 84, 87
Follman, J. F., Jr., 75
Food and Drug Administration, 162
Fragmentation, 169-71
Francis, Anita, 80
Fraud, 44
Freidson, Eliot, 20, 44, 98, 108, 114
Fried, Charles, 21, 101
Friedman, Lawrence M., 58, 109
Friedman, Meyer, 28, 143
Fuchs, Victor R., 14, 25, 44, 112, 129
Fullerton, Donald T., 84

Gardner, Elmer A., 81
Geertsen, Reed, 154
Ginzberg, Eli, 7
Glaser, William A., 112
Glass, Albert J., 152
Glasscote, Raymond M., 52, 60
Goals, conflicting, 28-29
Goldberg, Irving D., 84
Gray, Robert, 154
Greenberg, Bernard G., 16, 156
Greenley, James R., 80, 151
Grievance procedures, 117, 118-19
Grossman, Michael, 40
Group-practice situation, 44
Gudeman, Jon, 52, 60
Gurin, Gerald, 151

Haggerty, Robert J., 12, 29, 137
Havighurst, Clark C., 38-39
Health, Education, and Welfare
   (HEW), Department of, 26, 162
Health-belief model, 30-31
Health Care Financing Agency, 162
Health education, 25-28, 138-39, 152
   behavior models in, 30-33
Health and illness behavior, 16,
   146-58

adolescents and, 33, 34-36
barriers to individual responsibility,
   37
changing, 12-14, 25-37
children and, 33-35
community regulation and, 29
concepts of health and disease,
   147-49
conflicting goals and needs, 28-29
contextual demands on behavior,
   29-30
as coping mechanism, 156-57
determinants of, 153-54
development of, 33-36
distress, vocabularies of, 155-56
methods of studying, 149-53
models in health education, 30-33
socialization and, 35, 36, 154-55
unreliability of information, 27-28
Health insurance: *see* Coinsurance;
   Consumer choice; National health
   insurance
Health-maintenance organizations
   (HMOs), 14, 46, 59, 96, 111-12,
   114, 129, 135, 163
Health-services research, 18-19,
   125-36
analytic research and hypothesis
   testing, 31, 128, 131-32
demonstration and diffusion, 125,
   128, 134-36
evaluation research, 132-33
information and intelligence,
   130-31
policy analysis, 133-34
role of, 127-30
vulnerability of, 126-27
Heart surgery, 51, 172, 175
Hemodialysis, 51
Hetherington, Robert W., 20, 97, 110
Hip replacement, 51
Hollingshead, August B., 116
Homemaker services, 59
Hopkins, Carl E., 20, 97, 110
Hospices, 13
Human experimentation, 166
Hypertension, 138, 144, 149
Hypothesis testing, 31, 128, 131-32

Illich, Ivan, 25
Illness behavior: *see* Health and illness
   behavior

Imboden, John B., 156
Immunization, 12, 149
Implicit rationing, 19–20, 21, 95–98
Incentive reimbursement programs,
    96–98
Incompetence, 44
Indian Health Service, 161
Inflation, 6
Insomnia, 16, 80, 147
Institute of Medicine, 13, 110
Institutionalism, 52, 54, 66–67
Interest groups, 165, 166
Irish patients, 154
Italian patients, 154

Janis, Irving L., 32, 42
Jenkins, C. David, 143
Jewish patients, 154
Jogging, 27, 28

Kadushin, Charles, 156
Kagan, Jerome, 36
Kalton, Graham, 80
Kane, Robert L., 154
Katz, Harvey P., 37
Keairnes, Harold W., 94
Kerckhoff, Alan C., 156
Klarman, Herbert E., 38, 93
Klauber, Melville R., 154
Klein, Susan D., 115
Klerman, Gerald L., 143
Knowles, John, 25, 128
Krantz, Goldie, 84

Labor, Department of, 162
Labor unions, 160, 162, 166
Lasagna, Louis, 111
Last, J. M., 125
Lave, Lester B., 11
Leaf, Philip J., 71
Lefton, Mark, 52
Lejeune, Robert, 156
Leventhal, Howard, 32, 144, 149
Lewis, Charles E., 6, 28, 35, 79, 94,
    125, 126, 129, 150, 153, 167
Lewis, Mary Ann, 28, 35, 150
Ley, P., 13, 42
Librium, 81
License, suspension of, 108
Life-sustaining medical technologies,
    51

Linn, Lawrence, 70
Lion, Joanna, 80
Locke, Ben Z., 84
Logan, R. F. L., 100
Lohrenz, Francis N., 84
Long-term care, 9, 51–63, 144
    defining goals of, 53–55
    fragility of organizational
        alternatives, 60–62
    high-priority research areas in,
        62–63
    stability in funding, 56–60
Luikart, Clark, 17
Lynch, James J., 140

Maddox, George L., 17, 148
Malpractice, 44, 117, 118
Mandatory continuing education, 108
Manheimer, Dean I., 81
Mann, Leon, 32, 42
Market, as effective allocative
    mechanism, 91–92
McBroom, William H., 33
McKeown, Thomas, 11, 13
Meals on wheels, 59
Media, 28, 31
Medicaid, 6, 52, 54, 56, 65, 69, 79,
    109, 161, 162, 166
Medi-Cal, 111
Medical checkups, 149
Medical education, 115
Medical marketplace, 8, 38–47
Medical schools, 167–68
Medicare, 6, 17, 52, 54, 56, 65, 79,
    100, 105, 161, 162, 166
Mellinger, Glen D., 81
Mental illness, 9
    deinstitutionalization, 64–74, 144,
        174
    national health insurance and,
        75–88
Miles, Donald G., 52, 60
Milgram, Stanley, 102
Miller, Neal E., 144
Mormons, 29, 154
Murphy, George E., 81
Myers, Evelyn S., 76

National Academy of Sciences, 78
National Center for Health Services
    Research and Development, 162
National Center for Health Statistics,

130, 162
National Commission for Manpower
Policy, 17
National health insurance, 9, 21, 38,
39, 164, 165
critical isues for, 85–88
mental-health benefits under, 75–88
National Health Service of Great
Britain, 8, 59, 96, 100, 170
National Institutes of Health, 162
National Kidney Foundation, 102
National Library of Medicine, 162
National Research Council, 125–26
Nurse practitioners, 14, 135
Nursing homes, 17, 54, 56, 58–60, 65,
70, 144
Nutrition, 26, 32, 137, 138
Nycz, Gregory R., 84

Ombudsmen, 117, 119–20
Organ donation, 115, 116

Pain, responses to, 154, 156
Palmore, Erdman, 17
Parry, Hugh H., 81
Pasamanick, Benjamin, 88
Passivity, 36
Patients: *see also* Patients' rights
consumer choice, 38–47
health behavior: *see* Health and
illness behavior
physicians, relationship with, 41–44,
97, 99
Patients' rights, 104–21
approaches to accountability,
117–21
autopsy, 115, 116
conflicts in values, expectations, and
incentives, 112–13
consent, 115–17, 120
inequalities between providers and
patients, 113–15
organ donation, 115, 116
professional behavior of providers,
107–109
rationing: *see* Rationing
Patrick, Donald L., 82
Peer review, 44, 108
Perkoff, Gerald, 15
Physician assistants, 14, 15
Physicians
ambivalence toward, 36

capitation, 19, 20, 57, 59, 60, 69,
85, 98
cost sharing and, 19, 38, 39, 76, 77,
84, 92–95, 161
distribution of, 6, 168
ethical issues: *see* Ethical issues
fee listings, 43–44, 45
patients, relationship with, 41–44,
97, 99
peer review, 44, 108
primary care, 5, 6, 168, 170–71
Planned Parenthood, 17
Planning, 5, 173
Pless, Ivan B., 137
Policy analysis, 133–34
Prejudice, 107
President's Commission on Mental
Health, 82
President's Science Advisory
Committee Panel (1972), 18, 126
Pressman, Jeffrey L., 169
Prevention, 8, 11–13, 149
Price competition, 39
Primary-care physicians, 5, 6, 168,
170–71
Production of services, cost
containment and, 14–15
Professional standards review
organizations, 7, 108, 162, 165
Psychiatric care, insurance and, 75–88
Psychiatric need, 79–84
Psychoactive drugs, 64, 80–82, 139,
142, 144, 174
Public Health Service, 161
Public-interest lawyers, 102

Rabin, D., 14
Rationing, 10–11, 19–22, 91–103,
109–12
cost sharing as means of, 92–95
explicit, 20, 21, 98–101
implicit, 19–20, 21, 95–98
justice in, 110
market as allocative mechanism,
91–92
public role in establishing priorities
in, 101–103
Reed, Louis, 76
Reform, 7, 159–75
Reif, Laura Jean, 158
Reinhardt, Uwe E., 15
Reinholds, Harold, 96–97
Relaxation therapy, 142
Relicensing, 108

Richards, N. David, 25
Right to health care, 4
Rindflesh, Mark, 154
Robert Wood Johnson Foundation, 159
Robertson, Leon S., 12, 139
Robins, Lee N., 144
Roemer, Milton I., 20, 97, 110
Rogers, Everett M., 62
Roghmann, Klaus J., 137
Rosengren, William R., 52
Rosenhan, D. L., 75
Rosenman, Ray H., 28, 143
Rosenstock, Irwin M., 30, 31, 149

Salaried physicians, 113, 114
Sarason, Seymour B., 60
Schachter, Stanley, 155
Scheidemandel, Patricia L., 76
Schizophrenia, 82, 145, 153
Scull, Andrew T., 64, 66, 79
Segal, Steven P., 67, 72, 144
Self-esteem, 34
Self-help, 16, 17, 19, 140, 142
Seligman, Martin E. P., 54, 143, 148
Seskin, Eugene P., 11
Seventh-Day Adventists, 29
Sex differences, 150, 155
Sheltered living situations, 66
Shepherd, Michael, 80
Silver, Laurens H., 120
Simmons, Richard L., 115
Simmons, Roberta G., 115
Smits, Helen, 59
Smoking, 26, 28–30, 33, 137, 138
Social integration, 140–41
Socialization, 35, 36, 154–55
Somatization of psychological distress, 34
Specialists, 6, 168
Spector, K., 14
Spelman, M. S., 13, 42
Steele, James L., 33
Stein, Leonard I., 55, 68, 71, 83, 88
Stotsky, Bernard A., 54, 67
Strauss, Anselm L., 111
Stress, 26, 141–42
Stunkard, Albert J., 30
Suchman, Edward A., 154
Sudnow, David, 111

Suicide, 81
Supply and demand, concepts of, 40
Suspension of license, 108
Symptoms, interpretation of, 151–53
Szasz, Thomas S., 75

Technologic imperative, 14
Technology, 125, 134–36, 139, 172, 174
Tertiary-care facilities, 114
Tessler, Richard, 41, 45, 80, 148, 155
Test, Mary Ann, 55, 68, 71, 83, 88
Thalidomide, 166
Thomas, Lewis, 18
Titmuss, Richard M., 144
Townsend, Peter, 17
Tranquilizers, 81
Transplantation, 175
Truth telling, 109, 111
Type A personality, 143

Unionizion, 71
University psychiatry departments, 69

Valium, 81
Veterans Administration hospitals, 161
Volunteer services, 60

Warner, Kenneth E., 26
Wechsler, Henry, 33
Weil, Robert J., 66, 153
Weisbrod, Burton A., 68
Weissman, Myrna M., 143
White, Kerr L., 16, 156
Wildavsky, Aaron, 169
Williams, Allan F., 33
Williams, Kathleen N., 15
Williams, T. Franklin, 16, 156
Wing, J. K., 53, 66, 152
Women, 150, 152–53, 156
Worthington, William, 120

Youth peer groups, 33, 34

Zborowski, Mark, 154–55, 156